—NOTORIOUS— ANTEBELLUM NORTH ALABAMA

JOHN O'BRIEN

THE History PRESS

Published by The History Press
Charleston, SC
www.historypress.com

Cover images courtesy of Erica Lane.

First published 2020

Manufactured in the United States

ISBN 9781467141116

Library of Congress Control Number: 2020934444

CONTENTS

Contents

ACKNOWLEDGEMENTS

The following people have been integral to this book: My mother, Kay, for literally everything. My wife, Katherine, who has been an editor and confidant. My close friends and family, for assuming I would turn out all right and then making sure I did. And our fearless illustrators, Sha-Meika Smith and Erica Lane.

Brandy Panagos, for telling a weird kid he was good at writing. Nelda Newell, for giving me the only *F* I ever cared about. Christine Sears, for giving me the only *A* I ever felt I earned.

For my first fans, y'all were the only reason I wrote anything: Luis Felipe Salcedo Herrera, Elisabeth Spalding, Anton Larsson, Patrice Green, David Piersol and Jessica Barnett. Thanks to Jane DeNeefe and John McKerley, for giving me a part-time gig as a researcher. Additional feelings of gratitude to Ben Jobe and Daniel Bullard at Spice Radio, for producing the *Huntsvillain Podcast*.

The true foot soldiers of this work were Shalis Worthy at the Madison County Special Collections, Richard White at the Madison County Probate Archives, Kevin Ray at the University of Alabama Special Collections, Meredith McDonough at the Alabama Department of Archives and History Special Collections and Clint Bagley at the Mississippi Department of Archives and History. A special thanks to the untold number of student receptionists who had the misfortune of talking to me on the phone. And to Ben Hoksbergen, who answered all of my panicked Facebook messages about Middle Woodland and Mississippian settlements in the Tennessee Valley.

Additional thanks to my editors at The History Press and all of the unnamed people who have given me encouragement over the years.

All the mistakes are my own.

Introduction

OVERVIEW OF MADISON COUNTY'S HISTORY

North Alabama's history far predates the first cabin of John Hunt or the creation of Madison County. For fourteen thousand years, the region attracted a variety of people. During the Paleo-Indian period, North Alabama became a focal point of early human activity in the Southeast. Clovis culture spearpoints occur in greater densities throughout the Tennessee Valley than in any other part of Alabama, and a distinctive Redstone fluted spearpoint developed in North Alabama or Tennessee and spread eastward to the Carolinas and west into Louisiana. The rich game and ready foraging within the Great Bend of the Tennessee River sustained a large hunter-gatherer population for about five thousand years.

The Archaic period brought massive change. The end of the Pleistocene Ice Age meant that the world warmed and glaciers retreated, and over thousands of years, the climate of North Alabama morphed from one reminiscent of modern Manitoba to the hot and humid environment found today. Along with this general warming, new tools, food sources and trade networks emerged across the continent. Flint and iron ore from North Alabama found itself exchanged for mica from the eastern part of the state and sandstone from Mississippi. Archaic settlements sprang up around riverbanks and coastal regions, where the warmer waters allowed a far greater variety of mussels and oysters to flourish than had been possible during the Ice Age. If the mammoth hunt served as the stereotypical enterprise of the Paleo-Indian, then tossing an empty shell on the midden characterized their Archaic descendants.[1]

The oysters could not last forever. During the later Archaic and early Woodland periods, Native diets were increasingly dependent on horticulture and early agriculture. People became tied to their gardens, and regionally distinct artifacts emerged. Unlike the Redstone fluted spearpoint that stretched from southern Appalachia to the Gulf Coast, this regionalism flourished around river basins and tighter clusters of settlements, expressing itself primarily through funerary practices and pottery sherds.

The Copena Mortuary Complex emerged throughout the Tennessee Valley by the Middle Woodland period and marked a drastic transition from preexisting Archaic settlements. Rather than cluster around riverbanks, Copena villages tended to be farther inland, near better soils. They produced intricate pottery and left behind copper jewelry. Even the name ascribed to them, Copena, is a portmanteau of copper and galena (a type of lead ore) and indicates the types of metals they used to decorate their graves. The Copena left behind fifty funerary mounds stretching from Tishomingo County, Mississippi, to Hardin County, Tennessee, to the Guntersville Basin in Marshall County, Alabama. These were smaller mounds than those built by the contemporary Hopewell culture in the Midwest. For example, the most elaborate individual grave uncovered from a Copena mound contained eight objects, while Ohio Hopewell grave mounds contained hundreds of pipes and, in one extreme instance, one hundred thousand freshwater pearls.[2]

After AD 500, the Hopewellian influence in the Tennessee Valley declined and the Copena culture began to split into two groups: the Flint River culture (eastern branch) and the McKelvey culture (western branch). The Flint River culture adopted Mississippian characteristics by 600, with settlements switching from a series of rounded huts to houses with rectangular floor plans and wall trenches. In contrast, the McKelvey culture began building Mississippian-style platform mounds by the mid-700s. For centuries, the Flint River and McKelvey cultures lived in the remnants of the Copena complex, their artifacts capturing the gradual replacement of the Hopewell by the Mississippians as the dominant force of the Mississippi Basin.

By 800, all the settlements in North Alabama expressed significant Mississippian influence: traditional pottery-making practices that used limestone to temper ceramics gave way to shell-tempered ceramics with increasingly ornate features like loop and strap handles. The mounds changed, the pottery changed and the houses changed, marking a serious cultural shift. Mississippians built two mounds on Hobbs Island and settlements on Tick Island, a small island in Lawrence County destroyed by TVA dam projects in the 1930s. During the early Mississippian period, North Alabama developed close cultural ties to the large Moundville settlements on the Black Warrior River. Rock art reminiscent of the Southeastern Ceremonial Complex is located in caves on Redstone Arsenal. The Southeastern Ceremonial Complex was a series of symbols, characters and motifs that pervaded Mississippian sites throughout the southeastern United States.

Yet the settlements in North Alabama continued to shrink in size during the Mississippian period due to climatic factors. By 1500, people abandoned much of northern Alabama and central Tennessee due to a prolonged drought that decimated their crops and drove most of them from their homes and east into the Guntersville Basin or west toward the city-state of Chicaza. By the time Hernando de Soto traipsed through the Southeast, the area existed as more of a frontier between larger Mississippian kingdoms than as a distinctive region in its own right. In fact, de Soto originally followed the Tennessee River southward, but on reaching the Guntersville Basin, his expedition learned that few towns lay farther west and decided to turn southward into the chiefdom of Tuscaluza.[3]

The diseases de Soto and other conquistadors unwittingly unleashed destabilized most large southeastern Native communities. Throughout the 1520s, conquistadors prodded the maritime edges of North America; Juan Ponce de León and Pánfilo de Nárvaez launched their forays into Florida, while Lucas Vázquez de Ayllón explored the Georgia and South Carolina coasts. Trade between the sea and the hinterland flourished during the Mississippian period, and tragically, European and African diseases traveled into the interior as readily as seal skins and decorative shells.[4]

Two decades later, Tristán de Luna's short-lived colony near Pensacola recorded abandoned towns around the Alabama River, where de Soto found thriving farming villages. The Spaniards, low on food, took shelter among these ruins while waiting for resupply ships from Mexico. Once de Luna abandoned his designs in Pensacola Bay, the interior Southeast remained outside the immediate concern of European powers and their coastal outposts for decades. During the 1620s, Spaniards launched a handful of further *entradas* into La Florida, but increasingly, the Spanish exploration of the interior fell to Franciscan monks, a group more interested in building missions in the Panhandle than subjugating the Mississippian city-states along de Soto's original route.[5]

When Europeans finally returned to the interior, it was for its cheap deerskins and enslaved people. For a century, the Southeast experienced turmoil as groups raided one another to supply European coastal outposts with enslaved enemies. Bands roamed far and wide, coalescing and reforming into new societies along the way. Iroquois raided as far south as the Mississippi Valley, and Chickasaws traveled all the way to the Great Lakes in search of unguarded villages and deer.

By 1720, the peoples of the independent towns and neutral groups had either fled the region, joined with one of the major slaving societies, formed their own confederations for protection or sought shelter at European forts. These strategies were adopted by the most famous Native groups in Alabama: the Cherokee retreated from the worst of the violence in South Carolina and moved farther into the Appalachian Mountains, eventually establishing towns in the northeastern corner of Alabama; the Creek Confederacy began to take shape during the middle of the seventeenth century in response to raids from the Westos and the Chisca; in turn, the Choctaws banded together and developed close ties with early French explorers to better protect themselves from English-allied raiders; and the Chickasaws, whom English "Indian Dealers" sought out as early as the 1690s, replenished their population by absorbing refugees and adopting enslaved people from their own raids.

Of course, no one group existed as solely victims or victors, raiders or raided. The Creeks formed in response to slave raiding but soon launched their own raids deep into central Florida. The Chickasaws may have been one of the most formidable powers of the Mississippi Valley, but they also suffered attacks by the Osage and the Choctaw. Every Native nation utilized whatever strategy led to survival; they just leaned more heavily on select strategies.[6]

North Alabama remained contested for centuries, existing at the northern edge of the Creek Confederacy, the eastern edge of the Chickasaw homeland and the southwestern edge of the Cherokee settlements. Each group counted a portion of it as their hunting grounds. Gradually throughout the eighteenth century, the Cherokee pushed the Creeks farther south below the Tennessee River. By the time of the American Revolution, Madison and Jackson Counties existed as a borderland between the incoming Cherokee and the established Chickasaw.

After the 1720s, the Native slave trade tapered off as African captives filled the demand for unfree labor. The supply of deer, stressed by a century of nonstop hunting and leather production, withered in the region. Throughout the rest of the eighteenth century, the Natives of the Southeast found themselves trapped in a cycle of debt—unscrupulous English and Anglo-American traders proved more than willing to offer European trade goods on easy credit—yet there were not enough enemies or deer left to satisfy the debts. Increasingly, the Natives paid off their creditors by making concessions of land.

In 1783, when the United States signed the Treaty of Paris and became an independent nation, individual states still possessed conflicting claims with one another. Connecticut had a "Western Reserve" in northeastern Ohio. Virginia claimed lands that encompassed all of Kentucky and stretched north to Michigan. New Hampshire and New York each claimed the territory between them, which promptly seceded from both and reentered the nation as the state of Vermont.

Two states claimed land in what became North Alabama: South Carolina and Georgia. South Carolina, like most other states, ceded its western strip to the federal government in the late 1780s. Georgia, the youngest and brashest of the original thirteen colonies, refused to cede its western lands and, in 1794, organized a series of controversial sales of the Yazoo Lands (most of modern-day Mississippi and Alabama) to four land-speculation companies: the Georgia Company, the Georgia Mississippi Company, the Upper Mississippi Company and the Tennessee Company. Each of the companies paid around a penny an acre. Many Georgia state legislators participated in the running of the companies and attempted to enrich themselves from the land sales. In 1795, the backlash forced those who approved of the sales from political office, and the new members of the state legislature attempted to rescind the laws allowing the land sales. In the year between the first land sales and Georgia's attempted negation, much of the land had already been sold to third parties, resulting in a complex legal quagmire that led directly to Georgia ceding all of its western claims in 1802.[7]

Border drama on the Gulf Coast resulted in Spain ceding the most northern portion of its Florida claims in 1795. Three years later, Congress organized this area as the Mississippi Territory and, in 1804, added the adjacent Yazoo Lands. In 1805, the United States signed a treaty with the cash-strapped Chickasaw Nation, offering to pay off $20,000 in debt to its creditors in exchange for a long strip of land stretching from modern-day Paducah, Kentucky, to a triangular cross section in the Great Bend of the Tennessee River.[8]

Later that year, a man named John Hunt and his two sons finished building a cabin near a spring. They were not the first white settlers in the territory that became Madison County; the Criner brothers already had a

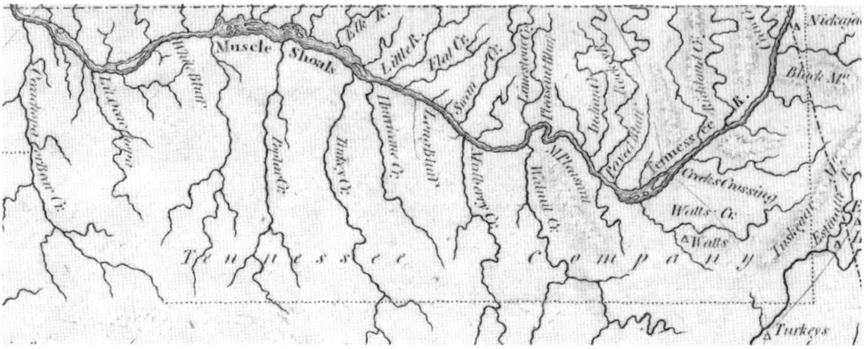

1804 map of the Mississippi Territory. *Courtesy of the W.S. Hoole Special Collections.*

cabin around New Market, and they furnished John Hunt with fresh bread on his first visit in the fall of 1804. James Ditto and his family operated a ferry across the Tennessee River for years before Hunt ever crossed the Tennessee state line. Nor would any of these people have been the first whites in the region. The expedition of Hernando de Soto skirted the Guntersville Basin and Great Bend of the Tennessee 264 years prior to John Hunt's first reconnaissance, while English slave traders ventured here to contact the Chickasaws as early as the 1690s.

Nor was it beyond the reach of most to travel farther inland. A trail ran from Winchester, Tennessee, to the state line. During the first decade of the nineteenth century, the Mississippi Territory slowly transformed into a land of roads; a portion of the Natchez Trace cut through the northwest section of the new territory, and to the south the Federal Road would soon connect a series of Creek trading paths to more established roads in the Carolinas, transforming a backwoods route into a direct line from Washington, D.C., to New Orleans.[9]

The land that John Hunt, the Criners and James Ditto colonized was not an unsettled wilderness but a carefully managed hunting ground on the border between sovereign Native nations. For over ten thousand years, the land that became Madison County had already hosted waves of settlers from across North America and seen city-states rise and kingdoms fall only to ascend again. European powers explored and exploited it for centuries before the first wave of American colonizers followed the Hunts, the Criners and the Dittos south. They did not find a frontier; they brought one with them.

The imported frontier filled in quickly. Within three years of John Hunt's cabin sprouting next to the Big Spring, letters flowed regularly between Natchez and Washington, D.C., about the future of the recently purchased Chickasaw lands. In one, dated August 23, 1808, Robert Williams, the governor of the Mississippi Territory, wrote to Albert Gallatin, the secretary of the treasury, about the massive influx of squatters. By his best estimate, thirteen hundred families resided within the Great Bend of the Tennessee. Worse, they already had "six or seven hundred militia organized into companies & armed." Governor Williams explained to Secretary Gallatin that because these settlers were "intruders," he possessed no real power over them. There were no local courts, land surveyors, justices of the peace, tax collectors or any other formal authority that linked these well-armed clusters of log cabins to the power brokers in Natchez. They were an authority unto themselves, and Governor Williams feared that unless he acted to establish order, "that quarter will become an asylum for the lawless."[10]

Secretary Gallatin presented these concerns to President Thomas Jefferson, who decided to let the settlers remain, so long as none of them based their land claims on fraudulent purchases from the Tennessee Company or had anything else to do with the Yazoo scandals. The president decided that Governor Williams possessed the authority to appoint officers for the previously lawless triangle. On December 13, 1808, Williams issued a proclamation describing a new division of the Mississippi Territory. To prevent "crimes and injuries" among the "several thousand Inhabitants having as yet no laws or officers," the lands south of the state of Tennessee, but north of the Tennessee River, east of the Cherokee Nation and west of the Chickasaw Nation should all be bundled into "one county, to be called and known by the name of Madison."[11]

The new American outpost grew quickly. In 1809, as part of the effort to establish order among so much perceived chaos, local authorities conducted a census. The 1809 Squatter List revealed a population on the move. Whereas a handful of Anglo-Americans resided within the bounds of the 1805 Chickasaw Cession when John Hunt first ventured there, just four years later, 2,223 free whites and 332 enslaved people called Madison County their new home. The earliest colonizers were not the ambitious single men associated with the frontier—those came later. The first wave of Americans consisted primarily of families. They poured over the border from Tennessee, drawn from the backwoods of Appalachia by the promise of good land recently wrested from the Natives. They squatted in the new county in the hope their claim might deter others from purchasing the plot they desired when land sales began in 1810.

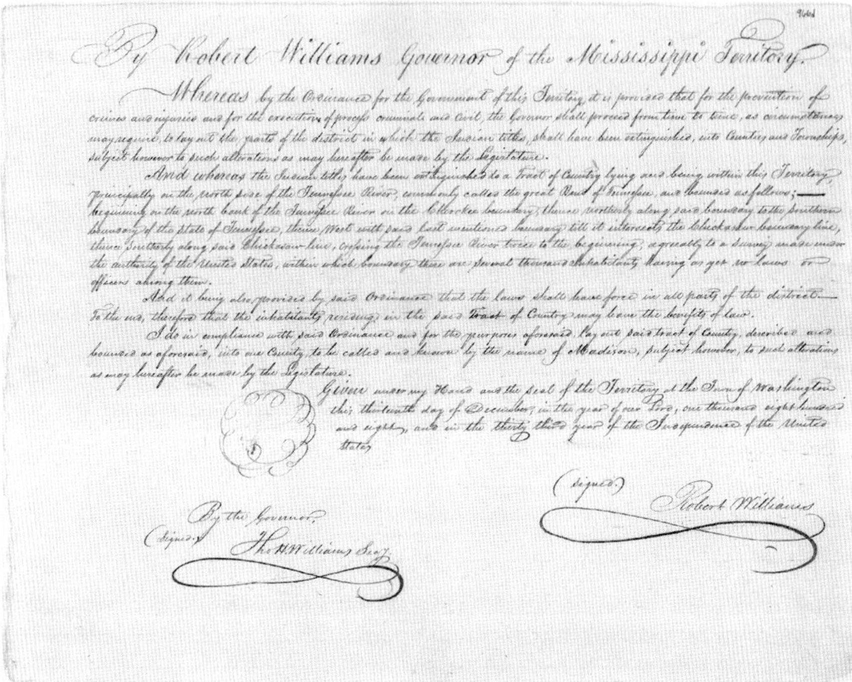

By Robert Williams Governor of the Mississippi Territory.

Whereas by the Ordinance for the Government of this Territory it is provided that for the prevention of crimes and injuries and for the execution of process criminal and civil, the Governor shall proceed from time to time, as circumstances may require, to lay out the parts of the district in which the Indian titles shall have been extinguished, into Counties and Townships, subject however to such alterations as may hereafter be made by the Legislature.

And whereas the Indian titles have been extinguished to a Tract of Country lying and being within this Territory principally on the north side of the Tennessee River, commonly called the great Bend of Tennessee, and bounded as follows;— beginning on the north bank of the Tennessee River on the Cherokee boundary, thence northerly along said boundary to the southern boundary of the State of Tennessee, thence West with said last mentioned boundary till it intersects the Chickasaw boundary line, thence Southerly along said Chickasaw line, crossing the Tennessee River twice to the beginning, agreeably to a survey made under the authority of the United States, within which boundary there are several thousand inhabitants having as yet no laws or officers among them.

And it being also provided by said Ordinance that the laws shall have force in all parts of the district— To the end, therefore that the inhabitants residing in the said Tract of Country may have the benefits of law.

I do in compliance with said Ordinance and for the purposes aforesaid, lay out said tract of Country, described and bounded as aforesaid, into one County to be called and known by the name of Madison, subject however, to such alterations as may hereafter be made by the Legislature.

Given under my Hand and the Seal of the Territory at the Town of Washington this thirteenth day of December, in the year of our Lord, one thousand eight hundred and eight, and in the thirty third year of the Independence of the United States

(signed) Robert Williams

By the Governor,
(signed) Tho H. Williams Secy.

Creation of Madison County. *Courtesy of the Mississippi Department of Archives and History.*

Even before the first official land sales, Madison County began its transformation into a hive of early industry. The 1809 Manufacturing Census measured economic indicators for each county within the Mississippi Territory. The government in Natchez counted extractive industries like the amount of cotton cloth, linen and wool produced. However, it also maintained an interest in the products of skilled labor, capital and artisans, like the number of looms, carding machines and distilleries present and the quantity of tin manufactured. Although Madison County existed for less than a year at the time of the census, it already had more looms than any other county and four of the six licensed distilleries in the Mississippi Territory. The following year, a territory-wide census showed that Madison County held the second-highest population. Only prosperous Adams County—which contained the capital city of Natchez, a well-established plantation regime and a bustling port on the Mississippi River—managed to surpass the rapidly growing Madison County.[12]

Land sales began in Nashville in 1809, and the raw potential of the young county attracted a variety of wealthier settlers, land speculators and investors. Due to the distance between the county and the land offices in Tennessee, many of the settlers who had petitioned Governor Williams for the protection of a local government and the creation of the county were subsequently forced off their new homes by factions of wealthy men. It was not until 1810 that a land office opened in Huntsville; by then, the choicest plots had been sold. The larger Nashville traders included Thomas Freeman (who originally surveyed the county), John Coffee and John Brahan. A second faction of wealthy men soon arrived from the Broad River area of Georgia.

The Broad River Group, also known as the Royalist faction, was a collection of wealthy interrelated families that migrated from Charlottesville, Virginia, to northeastern Georgia after the Revolutionary War. Once in Georgia, they established tobacco plantations around the confluence of the Broad and Savannah Rivers. From their base of operations at the tobacco inspection station in Petersburg, they saw the dwindling returns from tobacco and thought the fertile lands within the Great Bend of the Tennessee would serve as a suitable new home and investment. The Broad River Group included such notables as Alabama's first two governors, the brothers William Wyatt Bibb and Thomas Bibb;

Leroy Pope Mansion. *Courtesy of the Madison County Special Collections.*

future senator John W. Walker; Alabama's first federal judge, Charles Tait (who famously also had a peg leg); and Leroy Pope, who purchased all the lots that eventually became the new town of Twickenham.

The remaining squatters referred to the area that Pope purchased as Hunt's Spring, after John Hunt, and the name quickly became a symbolic point of contention between the newly arrived elites from Nashville and Petersburg and the stream of yeoman farmers from eastern Tennessee and North Carolina. In 1811, the yeomen managed to elect more of their representatives to the Mississippi Territory's legislature, and the name was soon changed to Huntsville.[13]

According to Judge Taylor's recollections of early Huntsville, the first court session took place in October 1810. Sheriff Stephen Neal marched into the courtroom, his sword drawn and held out before him. Judge Obadiah Jones followed. He wore a gown and a cocked hat with long plumes. The judge's sword hung from his waist. Contrary to Judge Taylor's recollections, a July term of the court had taken place, when squatters who had traded each other cattle and flour on credit came to sue one another over collections, but it appears these cases were not properly handled until January 1811. The July term, supervised by Leroy Pope, Thomas Bibb and John Withers, may have been more about the airing of grievances than actual legal recourse.[14]

Either way, an unbroken legal history of both Madison County and Twickenham (later Huntsville) began in 1810. By 1813, the *Madison Gazette* had published news of local jailbreaks and Andrew Jackson's exploits during the Red Stick War. By 1817, Huntsville had grown large enough to attract the attention of famous travel writer Anne Newport Royall, whose *Letters from Alabama on Various Subjects* provided detailed and lively depictions of the people of the Alabama Territory and early statehood.

In the summer of 1819, the city hosted Alabama's first constitutional convention. The president of the United States briefly visited. Someone brought an elephant and charged people fifty cents to watch it uncork wine bottles. In a decade, Huntsville was transformed from an unruly mob of militia and cabins into a destination where travelers brought the exotic.[15]

As Huntsville became more settled and the rough frontier decade of the Mississippi Territory (and its associated cheap land and ready opportunities) slipped away, the most ambitious settlers and land speculators started to drift from Huntsville and toward the recently ethnically cleansed parts of central Alabama. Obadiah Jones, the first circuit court judge for the northern section of the Mississippi and Alabama Territories, exemplified this trend. Although an important man in early Huntsville, by 1819, he had

Above: *First Court Date. Illustration by Sha-Meika Smith.*

Right: Portrait of Stephen Neal. *Courtesy of Alabama Constitution Hall Park.*

1819 elephant. *Courtesy of the Madison County Special Collections.*

advertised his plantation "locus in quo" for rent in the *Alabama Republican* and participated in the founding of the short-lived Marathon, also known as Melton's Bluff in Lawrence County.

By the mid-1820s, the seemingly exponential growth associated with boomtowns had dissipated. Although the earliest American colonizers were predominantly poor white farmers, by 1820, 49.3 percent of the population of Madison County consisted of enslaved Black people. In the decades immediately before the American Civil War, Madison County served as a microcosm of the whole state—unlike other predominantly rural and White counties in North Alabama, Madison County, with its majority enslaved population, resembled the plantation aristocracies of the Black Belt. Yet Madison County had the second-largest free Black population in Alabama and a relatively prosperous yeoman class, distinguishing it from counties like Montgomery, Wilcox and Greene.[16]

The original intent of this book was to present humorous and episodic accounts of early Madison County's strangest court cases. However, while researching, rewriting and arranging the contents contained herein, it became clear that not every episode would be humorous. Most are morose and horrifying. It is often impossible to deal fairly and accurately with the antebellum South, be a feeling person and chuckle, all at the same time.

Additionally, even though Madison County remained one of the largest population centers in Alabama through Reconstruction, the people existed in a much smaller and more intimate world. They did not rise and fall

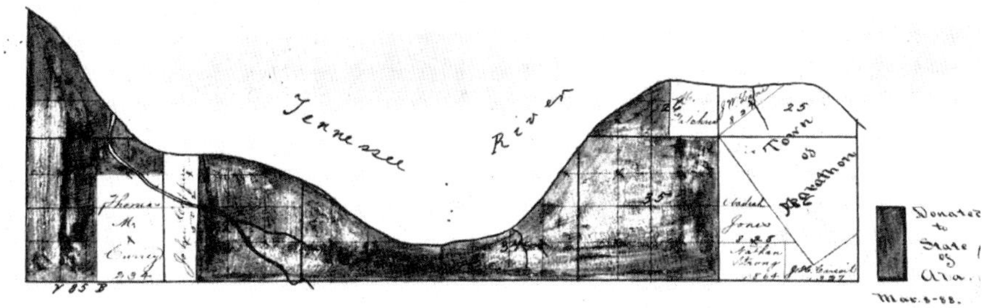

Above: Town of Marathon plat map. *Courtesy of the National Archives and Records Administration.*

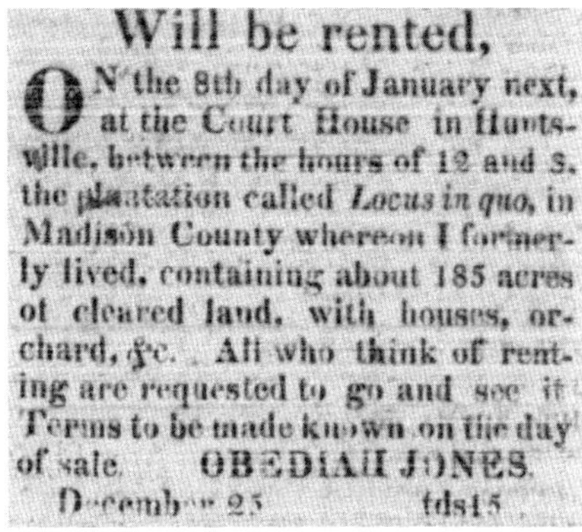

Will be rented,

ON the 8th day of January next, at the Court House in Huntsville, between the hours of 12 and 3, the plantation called *Locus in quo*, in Madison County whereon I formerly lived, containing about 185 acres of cleared land, with houses, orchard, &c. All who think of renting are requested to go and see it. Terms to be made known on the day of sale. OBEDIAH JONES.

December 25 tds15

Right: Obadiah Jones plantation for rent. *Courtesy of the Madison County Special Collections.*

away as the narrative demanded but reappeared in one another's lives as witnesses, jurors, murderers, assailants, thieves and lovers. Every class of person came before the court. But they did not do so proportionately. While enslaved people made up over half the population, they appear sparingly in court records with few descriptions. In the introduction to the chapter on hate crimes, I briefly discuss what seemed to be their conscious erasure by authorities.

All of the cases occurred between the 1810s and the eve of the American Civil War. During this time, Madison County transformed from a frontier on the northern fringe of the Mississippi Territory into the largest county in the state, briefly the site of its first capital and, finally, one large settlement among many.

This book has morphed from a collection of oddities into an examination of a specific time and place as it appeared to its least-examined citizens. Each section covers a category in chronological order to highlight changes in national attitudes and state laws. The astute reader will notice that most of the examined cases occurred between 1811 and 1823. This is not for lack of research. The frontier and early-statehood periods seemed to be the most exciting time to live in antebellum Madison County.

There are five categories of cases: assaults; murders; hate crimes; a miscellaneous category of liquor, kidnapping and prostitution; and divorce. I chose the cases for their fascinating qualities, bounty of documented evidence and the frequency with which townspeople appeared before the court. These are not typical cases, nor are they the only assaults, murders, hate crimes, kidnappings and divorces that happened in Madison County. They are exceptional instances representing the vivid yet incomplete whole. I hope reading the accounts contained herein provides insight into the earliest days of North Alabama but also produces empathy and understanding for the people who came before us. Feel free to laugh, recoil and mourn in equal measure. I know I did.

1
ASSAULTS

The Unfortunate Mr. Badger

On August 3, 1811, a man named John B. Haynes arrived at William Badger's home in the newly founded town of Twickenham. It was a Saturday night on the frontier. People prepared for the day of rest ahead of them. The records do not specify how deep into the evening it was when Haynes visited the "dwelling house." So, Badger and his family may have just finished dinner. Although court records from 1812 list him as a laborer and the 1812 Tax List says he paid only one dollar, in 1811, Badger was an artisan. At the time of Haynes's assault, everyone in town recognized William Badger as "a Silver smith" with his own home in the town itself. Records do not list John B. Haynes's motives for what came next.[17]

With a great fury, Haynes came down on the Badger household, which he "did violently and maliciously break, injure and greatly endamage." John B. Haynes pelted the structure with stones and sticks he found. Haynes tore Badger's "fence rails" out of the ground and swung them at the house. Badger's family members barricaded themselves inside.

The causing of terror rested on the mind of John B. Haynes. He braced himself against the frame and with his might "did break open the door." Once inside, he gazed upon Badger's cowering family and took to breaking all of their windows and committing "many other enormities" upon their home.

All this destruction proved insufficient for Haynes. He gazed upward, and an idea entered his mind. The family must have held tightly to one another as he left. Surely, their plight had ended. They would have heard John B. Haynes clamber onto the top of their home and watched in growing horror as he did violently "tear off the roof."

John B. Haynes, in contrast to the mildly prosperous artisan William Badger, was a much wealthier and controversial man. Although he spread terror as he went, Haynes was no simple thug. He did not steal from those he assaulted. Nor did he try to murder them. He attacked their property and usually avoided the consequences of the law.[18]

Haynes resided in Madison County long enough to appear on the 1811, 1812 and 1813 Tax Lists. He owned 160 acres of land on Indian Creek, in the southern part of the county, most likely near the Tennessee River and modern Redstone Arsenal. According to the 1811 Tax List, he had sold $3,000 worth of "merchandize" in the previous year. In 1812, he purchased ten enslaved humans.[19]

John B. Haynes leveraged himself into the role of a merchant and middleman. He often worked for the trading firm Calvin & Gideon Morgan, in addition to his private mercantile operations. Though the records are not always clear about what he sold, as a merchant, he appeared in at least twenty-two separate county court cases, most of them in 1813. These cases dealt primarily with debts promised but not paid. Haynes appeared as both plaintiff and defendant in equal measure and brought suits on behalf of both his private operation and of Calvin & Gideon Morgan.[20]

His mundane county court business dealings stand in contrast to his rowdy circuit court appearances. For instance, while already juggling multiple lawsuits in the county court, Haynes assaulted Badger again after having destroyed his home in August 1811. Additionally, on January 10, 1814, Haynes, an acquaintance named George Hays and six other unidentified men broke into Cary Bibb's house in Huntsville. They "did then and there destroy and injure the household furniture." Haynes exhibited a pattern of aggressive and willfully destructive behavior toward a handful of people but never raised a documented hand toward anyone who owed him money or was involved with his businesses.[21]

So, when Haynes tore the roof off of William Badger's house, he had no ulterior motives. He did not seek payment nor to influence Badger away from a court case. This was nothing less than pure, unyielding hatred and spite—emotions that William Badger seemed to inspire in people.

John Haynes briefly returned to the Badger residence after his initial rampage through their home. On August 10, a week from the day of the destruction of the roof, Haynes assaulted Badger again. This time, the records lack the destructive description of the previous encounter and rely more on rote phrases like "an assault did commit." So, although this second assault case lacks the panache of their first meeting, it confirms a continuing enmity between the two men.

On the same day that Haynes attacked Badger a second time, John J. Winston also made an assault on Badger. The records fail to indicate if Haynes and Winston made the assault together or if William Badger just had an awful day. What's more, his two assailants were fairly similar. Court records listed both men as merchants; they each made an assault on William Badger; and Winston later went on to assault additional people throughout Madison County. A case was dropped in November 1812 for an attack he made, alongside one Anthony Winston, against William Haskins.[22]

If Haynes and Winston did not know each other prior to their dealings with William Badger, they became acquaintances because of it. A July 1812 county court case listed both men jointly suing John Eckford for fifty dollars that Haynes had loaned to Eckford on December 28, 1811. It seemed several merchants were bound together in their distaste for the local silversmith.[23]

The assaults on William Badger continued. A man named Luther Morgan—once again, a local merchant—savaged Badger on an unspecified day in August 1811. By the time of Morgan's circuit court hearing in the spring of 1812, Badger had gone from being listed as a silversmith to a "labourer," suggesting a change in his fortunes since the first round of assaults by Haynes and Winston. For one reason or another, the assault charges against Luther Morgan were quickly "quashed," and he was allowed to go free.[24]

The last recorded assault occurred on August 16. For two weeks, men found and fought William Badger with such frequency that his life must have been a walking terror. Nicholas Gilbreath, his final assailant, was no stranger to violence. On April 20, 1810, he had assaulted, kidnapped and imprisoned a man named John Maxwell "for a long time to wit for the space of twenty Days." Gilbreath avoided prosecution on technicalities, and the jurors thought Maxwell's request for $1,000 in damages amounted to excessive fines. But Gilbreath was the type of man Badger seemed to encounter—wealthier than average, rough around the edges and out for blood.[25]

As for Badger himself, he resided in Madison County for a few years after the *mense horribilis* and even appeared in a handful of county court cases for mundanities like owing people money—not for extraordinary reasons like having his home and life slowly wrecked by a parade of merchants.

We know that after the second assault by Haynes, Badger fell in stature from silversmith to local laborer. Furthermore, a county court case from July 1813 shows that Badger never succeeded in rebuilding his home. As alleged in the 1813 case, around April 10, 1812, William Badger began boarding "himself & family" with Cullen Earp. According to the indictment, Earp took care of the "boarding, washing, lodging, diet, [and] drink" for the whole Badger clan for several months, and in that time, William Badger incurred a debt of sixty dollars.[26]

The chain of events set off by John B. Haynes's destruction of William Badger's house ruined the latter's property, livelihood and reputation. For the summer of 1811, Badger faced near constant abuse by merchants, some of whom were business partners or became business partners of Haynes. Badger and his family were forced into expensive lodgings with Cullen Earp, and the expense of court cases and lack of safety meant he could no longer ply his trade as a silversmith.

So, when, in the spring term of the court in May 1813, they both appeared on the same docket—Badger to answer for a separate debt of "thirty dollar six two and one half cents" he owed to William Wyatt, and Haynes to sue a man named Joseph Wofford on behalf of Calvin & Gideon Morgan—it must have been a tense time between them in the courtroom.[27]

THREE DAYS IN MARCH

For three days in March, their little war raged across the county.

The McMahan and Gibson families arrived in Madison County in the late 1810s and started feuding immediately. They left behind few traces aside from their violent court records.

The early nineteenth century, from the 1810s to the 1830s, saw nothing short of an exodus from the Atlantic Seaboard. White settlers spilled westward in a stubborn tidal wave of humanity fed by high birth rates, European immigration and a firm belief in Manifest Destiny. People did not dally long in a locale and, if they found few prospects, felt little apprehension about trying their luck elsewhere. Due to the transitory existence of the average White American on the frontier, it is rare to find troublemakers who put down stakes. So, although the Gibsons, McMahans and their various allies blazed across the Mississippi Territory in flashes of interlocking violence, they evaporated from Madison County's record books by the time of Alabama's first census. John McMahan, as the head of his household, appeared on the 1812 Tax List with no land and one enslaved person. A year later, his fortunes reversed when Madison County recorded him with 643 acres outside the Huntsville city limits.[28]

Prior to their appearances in the court records, none of the Gibsons appears on a tax list, suggesting they did not even have the shallow roots that the McMahan family had sunk into Madison County. Unfortunately, the motives of either group remain unclear. All that is known is it started with a simple assault.

On March 7, 1816, William Gibson and Philip Fields found William McMahan in Madison County. The records list both Gibson and Fields as yeomen and William McMahan as a simple laborer. These designations mean that both Gibson and Fields owned a small plot of land, while McMahan engaged in wage work for others. Additionally, Barnett Hicklin prosecuted all of the cases filed on William McMahan's behalf. A later suit identified Hicklin as a yeoman. So, the first assault may have occurred at Hicklin's farm, where William McMahan probably worked. Gibson and Fields confronted McMahan and "did then beat, wound, and batter." Both men were found guilty and fined for their actions. Gibson may have been the more violent of the pair, for, although Philip Fields paid a five-dollar fine, the jury decided that William Gibson should pay twenty dollars.[29]

Three days later, the McMahan family and its allies took revenge. They gathered their friends Henry Seeman and Barnet Hicklin, and together with them, the brothers McMahan—John, the injured William and Martin—descended on Robert Gibson while he was unawares. They did "riotously, beat, bruise and ill treat to the great damage of the said Robert."[30]

Both assaults took place in Madison County, though, unfortunately, the court documents fail to mention where. However, we can infer that everyone involved may have lived on the eastern edge of the county, because the next round of assaults took place on the same day within the Cherokee Nation, which lay on the northeastern edges of the Mississippi Territory.

William McMahan left from the assault on Robert Gibson in Madison County and then set out for the Cherokee lands to the east. He walked into a trap.

Byrd Ashburne and John Pate waited for William McMahan inside the bounds of the Cherokee Nation. Their involvement complicates the tale. They either heard of the assault on Robert Gibson and made a unilateral

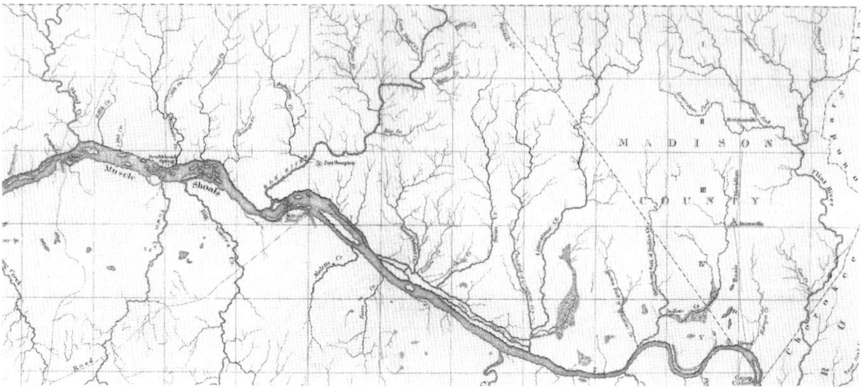

1817 map of Northern Alabama Territory. *Courtesy of the W.S. Hoole Special Collections.*

decision to strike at William McMahan, or they previously knew he would enter the Cherokee Nation at a specific time and had no qualms about ambushing him.

There are few direct links between Ashburne, Pate and the Gibson family. However, the immediacy of the ambush, their knowledge of where McMahan intended to be and the fact that Barnet Hicklin also sued Ashburne and Pate on McMahan's behalf point to a level of interconnectedness to the violence of early March 1816.[31]

When they found William McMahan, Byrd Ashburne grabbed his ten-dollar musket, which he "in both his hands then and there held" to threaten McMahan. John Pate stood nearby and "wickedly, willfully and of his malice aforethought" urged Ashburne to pull the trigger.

The bullet penetrated William McMahan "about an inch on the left side of the backbone," which left "one mortal wound of the depth of six inches & of the breadth of one inch." The two men fled after shooting him, but McMahan languished for three days before sliding into death—long enough to tell witnesses the exact facts of his murder.

Obadiah Jones barely knew what to do. What remained of the McMahan family, the Gibsons and their associated allies all crowded into his courtroom on the same Monday in May. Jurors for each case waited with all the patience of lawful busy men ready to make "true deliverance…between the Territory and the prizoners at the bar." Justice had to be swift.

The jurors heard each case and quickly issued a slew of fines commensurate to each man's share of the turmoil that had rolled across the county. They fined John McMahan nine dollars for beating Robert Gibson. Barnet Hicklin paid fifty dollars for his vicious attack on Robert

Gibson. The court acquitted Martin McMahan, Henry Seeman and John Pate on all charges.

Finally, it came to Byrd Ashburne, the only killer of the bunch. Jurors returned from deliberating over his sentence and deemed Ashburne "not guilty of murder but guilty of the felony of manslaughter." Due to the riotous nature of early March, he barely avoided a noose. Instead, he earned a twenty-five-dollar fine and four months "in the prison of said county."

ELK COUNTY CORN FIGHT

In May 1817, the Mississippi Territory created the short-lived Elk County. It lasted less than a year. In January 1818, the eastern sections of Elk County became the westernmost portions of Madison County and produced few memorable moments in local history—except that first Christmas.

On December 25, 1817, a fight broke out between three men "at the plantation & farm then occupied by Ezekiel Madkins within the County then known and established as the County of Elk." Although records do not list the exact location of the Madkins plantation, the fact that it was in Elk County, which would become the western portion of Madison County, and the existence of a contemporary Madkin Mountain indicate that the assaults probably took place on what is now the southern portion of Redstone Arsenal.

The fight itself was a vicious affair involving a local, well-respected laborer and two brothers from a powerful yet otherwise violent frontier family.

Prior to the affair on the Madkins plantation, Thomas Evans appeared on four separate juries in 1816 and early 1817, deciding the fate of his neighbors on issues like assault and selling liquor without a license. Although the court did not record his reason for being at Ezekiel Madkins' farm on Christmas Day, he probably worked for the man or was friendly with him and knew him. Court documents described John L. McGaha and Livingston S. McGaha as yeomen, so they owned land in the county. However, the first appearance of the McGaha family in local court records is in 1813, when Aaron and William McGaha stole a horse from Isaac Hinsly. William later escaped from the Huntsville jail and may have convinced a young enslaved man named Shadrick to run off with him.[32]

It was a peaceable enough day for both Thomas Evans and the Madkins plantation before the McGahas arrived.

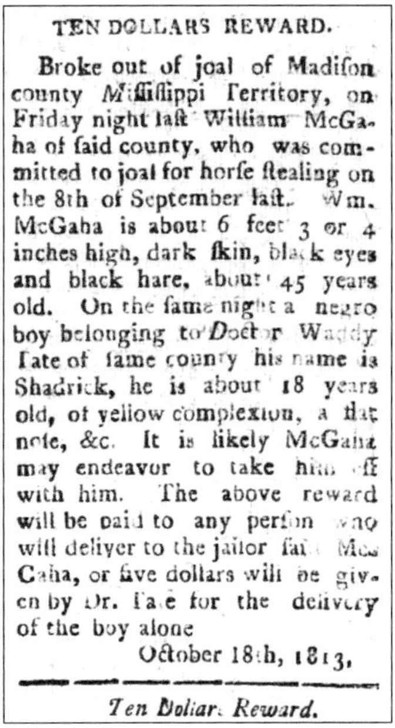

TEN DOLLARS REWARD.

Broke out of joal of Madifon county Miffiffippi Territory, on Friday night laft William McGaha of faid county, who was committed to joal for horfe ftealing on the 8th of September laft. Wm. McGaha is about 6 feet 3 or 4 inches high, dark fkin, black eyes and black hare, about 45 years old. On the fame night a negro boy belonging to Doctor Waddy Tate of fame county his name is Shadrick, he is about 18 years old, of yellow complexion, a flat nofe, &c. It is likely McGaha may endeavor to take him off with him. The above reward will be paid to any perfon who will deliver to the jailor faid McGaha, or five dollars will be given by Dr. Tate for the delivery of the boy alone

October 18th, 1813.

Ten Dollars Reward.

McGaha jail escape. *Courtesy of the Madison County Special Collections.*

Something happened that sparked a violent uproar. Thomas Evans attacked the McGaha brothers with his hands and feet and inflicted grave damage on them. They responded with whatever they had on hand, namely "sticks, ears of corn, fists and feet." Most assailants carried out their attacks with a club or a knife, occasionally beating people with a gun or shooting them, but the mention of sticks and corn imply that the McGahas may not have been prepared and did not go to the farm intending to fight.

The court came down harder on Evans. Although each man involved received assault charges, only Evans paid damages: $75 for his assault on John McGaha and an additional $100 fine for beating Livingston McGaha. The charges against Aaron and William McGaha were dismissed in 1820 and 1822, respectively. Their family likely went on to amass wealth—an 1840 map of Huntsville reveals a large McGehee reserve off of Holmes Avenue. In an ironic turn of events, they even assisted local constables in apprehending convicts who had escaped from the local jail. Thomas Evans faded from the court documents and never appeared on a jury again.[33]

CUTTING THE FIGURES AND VEINS OF SAMUEL BENNETT

A special enmity developed between Samuel Bennett and Richard Pryor in the early 1820s. It all began on a Monday in February 1820 and branched out into a series of assaults, bonds and cases that took three years for the circuit court to process. The one-sided violence that existed between the men—Richard Pryor always assaulted Samuel Bennett—is extraordinary because most of it can be explained. The majority of assault and murder cases that appeared before the circuit court seemed to come from the ether and return there. However, we can establish clear motives for each subsequent assault, and the violence builds to an actual conclusion. This brief window into a prolonged argument between two men lends itself well to a narrative.

The drama commenced on February 28, 1820, when Richard Pryor attacked Samuel Bennett "with hands and feet" inside the corporate limits of Huntsville. This was not Pryor's first appearance before the circuit court. In 1817, he answered a summons as to why on April 20 he "did aim point and attempt to shoot" a man named Ezekiel Bess. Luckily for Bess, the pistol, though loaded, misfired. Luckily for Pryor, the prosecution dragged the case out until 1820. Thus, the original "Attorney general of Madison County," Henry Minor, had moved on to another position. Joseph Eastland replaced him, though the job now bore the much less prestigious title of "solicitor." Eastland proved unwilling to finish prosecuting his predecessor's full caseload and, on March 6, 1820, appeared before the court, stating that he "does not wish to further prosecute the said defendant."[34]

Unchecked by the court the first time, Pryor felt little need to conceal the February 1820 assault on Bennett. The circuit court, once again delaying a minor assault involving Pryor, would not actually try the case until April 1822. They asked Pryor to issue a bond on March 17, 1820, pledging he would "keep the peace towards all the good citizens of the said State and especially towards Samuel Bennett" for the space of one year. He produced a second guarantor, likely a friend or business partner, named Thomas Cain. Together they pledged that Pryor intended to keep the peace until 1821. If he failed to keep his hands and pistols to himself, then he forfeited $500 to the county. Bonds like these proved common in nineteenth-century circuit court cases. The court hoped that, by forcing a defendant to draw on their own social networks to produce the exorbitant amount of money required by these bonds, their friends and family would monitor the defendant's conduct and that social pressure might prevent a relapse or further assault.[35]

However, Richard Pryor appeared to be a man unmoved by the constraints of social networks. Even the loss of his $500 bond, worth about $11,000 in contemporary cash, failed to faze him. Samuel Bennett had to suffer for reporting the first assault.

On August 25, 1820, Pryor assaulted Bennett near Huntsville. This time, he brought a pistol. Pryor, perhaps reminiscent of the failed murder of Ezekiel Bess, opted out of shooting Bennett. He flipped the weapon around and gave him "divers terrible grievous, and other dangerous blows" with the butt of the pistol. He focused his wrath on Bennett's head and face, which he "grievously cut, bruised, and wounded" as he attempted to cave the man's head in with a gunstock.

Bennett managed to briefly escape the fury of the man who intended to "kill and murder and [commit] other wrongs" on him. As Bennett staggered away from the vicious assault, Richard Pryor followed him. Pryor threatened Bennett that he would find him again, and the next time, he intended to "cut the figures & veins" of Samuel Bennett if he "refused to dismiss the suit" against him.[36]

The court was none too pleased with Pryor's behavior. It issued a writ of scire facias on February 5, 1821, which summoned him before the court to give an account of his actions and explain how he planned to pay off the $500 bond or why he should be exempt from the recognizance. Pryor delayed the proceedings for seven months. He either failed to appear or begged for an extension from the court. Finally, on December 7, 1821, Lemuel Mead, the court clerk, summoned him. Five days later, Sheriff Stephen Neal brought Pryor before the court to answer for his alleged crimes. It probably seemed a bleak time in his life, but the delays allowed Pryor to hire a good law firm. The attorneys from Kelly & Hutchison laid out the case that the court's directions proved vague. According to them, the slight differences between "keeping the peace" and pistol-whipping Samuel Bennett were great enough that the initial bond was void of substance.[37]

Surprisingly, this worked. In April 1822, the circuit court finally settled on a punishment for the February 1820 assault. The jurors found Pryor guilty but assessed his fine to the "sum of five dollars." At the same term, the court decided the bond proved too vague, so, instead of holding him to the $500 recognizance, they sided with the lawyers from Kelly & Hutchison. All that remained was to answer for his second, far more fearsome, assault on Bennett and the charge for contempt of court he received for threatening to cut out Bennett's veins.

On November 4, 1822, the jurors returned from their brief deliberation to announce that they indeed found Pryor guilty on the second count of assault. This time, they reasoned that the brutality of the violence and the premeditation inherent in trying to intimidate a witness warranted a more substantial fine. As such, they decreed that the governor of Alabama recover against Pryor "the sum of seventy five dollars"; they additionally ordered he remain in custody until the full sum was produced. There would be no delays followed by a slick team of shameless lawyers this time. The court decreed that Pryor should languish in the local jail until he repaid his debts to society. As such, the sheriff had no trouble finding him four days later. Pryor remained where Sheriff Neal had left him. The court questioned Pryor about his charge of contempt. He answered them in such a way that the court was "satisfied that he hath purged himself of said contempt" and earned himself an acquittal.

The years-long drama involving Samuel Bennett and Richard Pryor allowed an insight into the relationship between two different men—one never entered the court as a defendant, the other remained an eternal plaintiff. Bennett appeared in later circuit court cases, once again as the victim of violence, while Pryor may have finally internalized his brief brush with justice and quit assaulting people after languishing in jail until he could raise the seventy-five dollars needed to pay his fine. In a rare turn, this series of circuit court cases offers narrative and motive.

In early nineteenth-century court records, it is nigh impossible to tease out the reasoning behind the harsh and unyielding violence described. Yet here the court recorded the reasoning for the subsequent assaults clearly and without pretense. Pryor wanted something from Bennett, and he was willing to lose a great sum of money and torture another man to get it. The examination of violence through court records that have no recorded motive can make the acts feel random or sporadic. This series of cases highlights the fact that, outside of war, hate crimes and acts of genocide, violence rarely exists for its own sake and must be understood as another form of communication. Violence is a language that often touches those on the edges of our social circles. Pryor's continued viciousness toward Bennett is a reminder that, first, the record is always incomplete—diligence is required to tease out the specifics of the participants' lives—and second, even in nineteenth-century Alabama, you don't often pistol-whip someone you don't know.

WITH COWHIDES AND CONSTABLE COTTRELL

Huntsville lacked a regular patrol unit until October 12, 1831, when, in a direct response to the Nat Turner Rebellion of Southampton County, Virginia, the board of aldermen voted to hire a Night Watch. At ten o'clock each evening, the two officers of the Night Watch rang the courthouse bell and then patrolled the streets of Huntsville, where they arrested any free Blacks, enslaved people and "drinking white persons" found on the streets after curfew. Infrequent slave patrols existed prior to the institution of the Night Watch, but the patrols cared little for justice and spent time stamping out imaginary insurrections in the county. Constables conducted the functions of the court prior to 1831.

Constables differed from both the Night Watch and modern police units in that they were elected. Voters elected the town's constables until the board of aldermen amended the town charter in December 1829. As elected, and even unelected, public officials, they often filled a variety of roles unassociated with patrolling or keeping the peace. City ordinances reveal that Huntsville's constables were expected to act as "clerk of the Market," summon people to repair city streets, inspect fire hydrants for leaks, register the amount of gunpowder in each household and "kill any dog seen running at large." All of this in addition to their regularly scheduled duties like feeding prisoners and buying candlesticks for the board of aldermen meetings.[38]

Yet, for playing such a vital role in the enforcement of ordinances and functioning of the community, local histories rarely mentioned constables. However, a group of cases from 1821 and 1822, involving constable John A. Cottrell, reveals an existence wholly different from that of the long arm of local bureaucracy described by the city's statutes.

The excitement began over counterfeit money.

On July 16, 1821, Thomas Watson and Thomas Garner "feloniously did forge and counterfeit" a series of fifty-dollar "promissory notes" supposedly issued by the Bank of Tennessee. The inhabitants of early North Alabama shared a deep hatred for forgers and counterfeiters. James Gillespie Birney, an abolitionist who briefly lived in Huntsville and a lawyer with a soft streak for the dispossessed, represented a counterfeiter menaced by a "lynch club" in Jackson County in the early 1820s. On March 30, 1821, Martin Dunnegan forged grocery receipts at a general store owned by Luther Morgan. Dunnegan was hanged for the crime in September 1821. So, the accusations and ire directed toward the two men were no less than matters of life and death. Thomas Garner quickly disappeared from the record; either he possessed the ability to flee the county or a local "lynch club" menaced him into an early grave.[39]

It took the law several days to act. On July 20, four days after Thomas Watson "falsely made forged and counterfeited" notes, Justice of the Peace Robert W. Roberts issued a warrant for Watson's arrest. Cottrell quickly found Watson and apprehended him. However, while conveying Watson to the jail, Cottrell "unlawfully and negligently" permitted Watson to escape and "go at large whethersoever he would."

Cottrell handled Watson's escape the same way he appeared to handle other constabulary crises: by gathering a posse. On July 19, 1821, the day before he both arrested and lost Thomas Watson, Cottrell organized vigilante justice against Benjamin Camp. Camp appeared in no other records, so it is

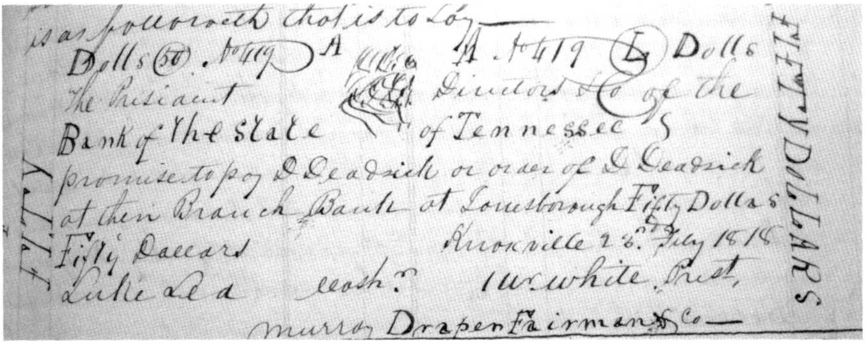

Counterfeit notes. *Courtesy of the Madison County Probate Archives.*

unclear if the circuit court ever charged him with a crime, yet he managed to attract the wrath of John Cottrell and his friends. The posse consisted of six men: John Morgan, Robert Jones, John Ingram, Armistead Jones, Thomas McGehee and John Cottrell. The men cornered Camp and proceeded to viciously assault him. They punched and kicked Camp until their limbs grew tired. Then, in a fit of violent inspiration, they incorporated what they had at hand into their rage. Glancing about them, they found the common fibers of their time. Now armed with hide and hawser, they beat Benjamin Camp with "Ropes and a cow skin."

It took four days to find Thomas Watson. For four days, Cottrell and his expanded posse hunted for the man. Three men reappeared in this second assault case: Thomas McGehee, Robert Jones and, of course, John Cottrell. The other members of the posse included Anthony Metcalf, Edward Morgan and Francis Morgan, as well as John McGehee, a probable relative of Thomas McGehee.

When all seven men finally found Watson, they fell upon him with the fury reserved for counterfeiters. On July 24, 1821, they beat him until "his life was greatly despaired of." Not content with their quotidian assault, one of the men who had been present at the beating of Benjamin Camp—Cottrell, McGehee or Jones—upped the ante by finding "a cowhide skin" and used it to lash and torture Watson.[40]

The fallout was immediate. The jury, though it had ample evidence to convict Thomas Watson in the form of multiple counterfeit bills, was moved by his plight and found him not guilty after a last-minute attempt by Joseph Eastland to drop the charges. As for the men conscripted into Cottrell's posse, jurors ultimately found most of them not guilty; only Thomas McGehee received a symbolic fine of "one cents" for the viciousness of his extrajudicial assault on Benjamin Camp. The brunt of the jury's ire rested squarely with John Cottrell, who received a fine of "thirty five dollars" for his abject failure of duty in allowing Thomas Watson to escape.

As eventful as July 1821 proved for Constable Cottrell, February 1822 would be worse. In the previous set of cases, Cottrell commanded the mob violence. But now, it was his turn to be hunted by vigilantes.

On February 11, 1822, Littleberry Lesseuer, a justice of the peace, settled an argument between two men. Lesseuer determined that Benjamin T. Saxon owed James Taylor "the sum of twelve Dollars and eighty one a fourth cents," along with adjudication costs of "one dollar and thirty one and a fourth cents," all $14.12½ to be collected by John A. Cottrell.

Cottrell carefully considered the property owned by Benjamin T. Saxon and settled on what he should take as either payment or collateral. Later the same day, he seized a "chesnut sorrel Gelding" from Saxon and took the horse to a stable owned by his relative Richard Cottrell. At this point, the records seemingly conflict with one another. Benjamin T. Saxon, John Stofford and Robert Chapman supposedly assaulted Cottrell and reclaimed the aforementioned horse on both February 13 and February 19. However, an examination of the court records indicates that it is likely a description of two separate events. Of the four separate cases detailing the back and forth between Constable Cottrell and Benjamin T. Saxon, only one mentions that they stabled the horse with Richard Cottrell. Two others described the February 19 conflagration, while the last is a $1,000 bond stating that the men would not seek retribution and appear before the court.

So, it appears that on February 13, the posse arrived at Richard Cottrell's stables, spotted the gelding and then "feloniously and violently did steal take and lead away" Saxon's horse. Incensed by this breach of contract, Cottrell took the horse again. Records listed the price of the gelding at $200, and Saxon rightfully refused to lose a horse of that stature to satisfy a debt of $14. On February 19, the posse returned; this time, they not only recaptured the horse but also went a step further. The three men assaulted the constable as he tried to stop their theft.[41]

Saxon, Chapman and Stofford appeared before the court on November 4, 1822. Saxon hired a local law firm, Henderson & Woodridge, to represent him. They argued that no records of the original orders existed and that Saxon was subsequently "not bound by the laws of the land" governing interactions between citizens and the constabulary. Jurors ultimately proved sympathetic to the men's plight and acquitted all involved.

Constable Cottrell faded from the record after these cases. The people of Huntsville elected other constables before the board of aldermen began appointing the position in 1829. However, his brief moments as the focus of the court's attention illuminated the relationships between the city and its citizens. As an enforcer of law and order, he proved uneven at best. It is difficult to imagine him beating any of his co-conspirators or their family members with cowhides, and his attempt to garrison Saxon's prized gelding horse at his relative's stable lends itself to suspicious interpretation. Memory of Cottrell's poor record, and blunders by later constables, may have inspired the aldermen to change the city's charter and assume direct oversight of Huntsville's slowly developing police force. As an elected official, Cottrell nominally served the people of Huntsville, but his actions in the early 1820s, like using extrajudicial violence to hide his mistakes and confiscating property not commensurate with fines levied by the courts, indicate that he mostly served himself.

2
MURDERS

Newman's Razor

On Friday, June 6, 1812, a murder took place. In the Chickasaw Nation, Eli Newman came upon Joseph Tetrick and slit his throat with "a certain instrument called a razor." Court records estimated its worth to be about one dollar. The wound, two inches deep and two inches wide, was truly ghastly. It caused Tetrick awful pain from which he "languished and [while] languishing did die."

The court rushed the prosecution. Murder trials, unless they occurred immediately before a regularly scheduled session of the court, often dragged on for years as the sheriff found witnesses and sufficient jurors. This murder caused Judge Obadiah Jones and Sheriff Stephen Neal to call a special session in December 1812, an unusual move prompted by the county's first murder case.

Eli Newman and his attorney, John W. Walker, mounted an impressive thirteen-point legal argument against his murder charge. The majority of defendants, even those tried for murder, simply pleaded not guilty and waited for their judgment; few possessed the tenacity to challenge the judge and jurors on the finer points of law.

In their unlikely rebuttal, Newman and Walker pored over the details of the case, disputing every procedural misstep taken by the territorial prosecutor Louis Winston, Judge Jones and Sheriff Neal in an attempt to have the case dismissed on a series of technicalities. Indeed, according to their twelfth point, they had already used this exact strategy to have the case thrown out twice. Newman complained that to bring him on the same murder charge a third time "impugns the sacred principals [*sic*] of the constitution."

As before, their legal defense swung at everything. They pointed out that they lacked all the facts pertaining to the case as "no copy of a caption of the indictment has been served on the traverser," that the indictment lacked basic information like "the depth of the wound" and that the original wording of the indictments only implied that Newman had committed murder. Indeed, according to Newman and Walker, much of the original evidence offered by Madison County rested on inference, "which in cases of blood the law abhors." The court took all of this into consideration, fixed its procedural errors and continued with the trial.

Doubtlessly frustrated by the proceedings but fighting for his life, Eli Newman began yet again. He dealt not with his own innocence—Newman never denied that he might have killed Joseph Tetrick—but repeatedly pointed out the location of the murder: the Chickasaw Nation. The third, seventh, eighth and ninth points of Newman's renewed legal defense all dealt specifically with the location of the crime and Madison County's lack of jurisdiction.

Newman alleged the original jury incapable of examining his case because the sheriff raised and elected the jurors "in and for the body of the county of Madison," and as the Chickasaw Nation existed wholly outside of Madison County, any jury raised within it could not find him guilty. Newman claimed that jurors raised by the county could not weigh his deeds, but also that the whole trial lacked credibility because Madison County did not possess the jurisdiction to try crimes committed in the Native nations found within the Mississippi Territory. He also stated that as "the place of death is not laid within the county," its courts had no right to even consider the case.[42]

It's true that the Chickasaw Nation in 1812 lay outside the bounds of Madison County, but American law considered Native nations subordinate to the states and territories they lay within, and the Chickasaw Nation overlapped with the northwestern quarter of the Mississippi Territory, the whole western third of the state of Tennessee and a fat triangular chunk of Kentucky.

However, the judges and juries in Huntsville heard cases from across the unorganized northern stretches of the Mississippi Territory all the time. They considered thefts in Blount County, assaults in the Cherokee

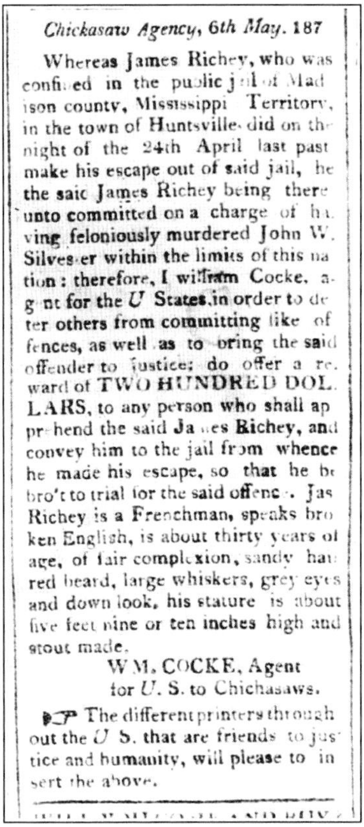

Chickasaw Agency, 6*th May*. 187

Whereas James Richey, who was confined in the public jail of Madison county, Mississippi Territory, in the town of Huntsville, did on the night of the 24th April last past make his escape out of said jail, he the said James Richey being thereunto committed on a charge of having feloniously murdered John W. Silvester within the limits of this nation: therefore, I william Cocke, agent for the *U* States, in order to deter others from committing like offences, as well as to bring the said offender to justice; do offer a reward of TWO HUNDRED DOLLARS, to any person who shall apprehend the said James Richey, and convey him to the jail from whence he made his escape, so that he be bro't to trial for the said offence. Jas Richey is a Frenchman, speaks broken English, is about thirty years of age, of fair complexion, sandy haired beard, large whiskers, grey eyes and down look, his stature is about five feet nine or ten inches high and stout made.

WM. COCKE, Agent
for *U*. S. to Chichasaws.

☞ The different printers throughout the *U* S. that are friends to justice and humanity, will please to insert the above.

Chickasaw Agency murder notice. *Courtesy of the Madison County Special Collections.*

Nation and even divorces from south-central Tennessee. The enforcement of laws beyond the borders of the county became old hat pretty quick. In fact, Newman's case was not even the only one in which the court asserted jurisdiction over the Chickasaw Nation during the November 1812 term. While Newman argued that the American courts had no jurisdiction over Chickasaw lands, jurors in Madison County indicted Samuel Steel for stealing a bay horse from Thompson Windham within the Chickasaw boundaries. The horse thief helped seal not only Newman's fate but also established precedence that affected later criminals as well.[43]

Eli Newman and his attorney presented a whole array of arguments dealing with jurisdiction, double jeopardy and decorum. But Judge Obadiah Jones and Sheriff Stephen Neal had all the power, the precedent and the rope. Judge Jones inspected his legal gambit and declared "that the said reasons are insufficient."

The jurors found him guilty, and on Saturday, December 5, 1812, "between the hours of ten in the forenoon and two in the afternoon," the sheriff led Eli Newman "to the place of execution," where the authorities he claimed lacked the power to sentence him hanged him by the neck until he was dead.

As the years passed, the county and the Native nations that bordered it saw more violence and gore. Yet most accused nineteenth-century murderers came, went and hanged with surprising timidity—as if already resigned to their fates. Eli Newman, the man at the center of the county's first murder case, fought the hardest and argued the longest of any of them while passively admitting to his crimes along the way.

EDMOND LESTER AND THE ELECTION OF 1823

They tried to lie to the courts. Andrew Lester and Winbush Lester saw that their relative might be hanged, and they closed ranks around him. When the judge asked if he had an alibi, they provided one. It might have worked if the lie had not been so bold nor the crime so heinous.

The Lester family lived near the Flint River, which rises in Lincoln County, Tennessee, and flows southward for sixty-five miles before meeting the Tennessee River south of Hobbs Island, near modern Cloud Cove. The land near it is flat and well-watered, perfect terrain for the succession of towns and unincorporated communities huddled around its forks and bends as it zigzags through western Madison County—places with fanciful names like Owens Crossroads, Moontown and Bell Factory. They all depended on the Flint River for water, power and transportation to the markets of the Tennessee River.

The Lesters were poor men on rich land.

Court documents list all the Lester brothers as "labourers," implying that they owned no land and sought a wage from working for others. The case against Edmond Lester does mention him having a house, so they may have owned a plot with no acreage or rented from a landlord. Nor do we know exactly when the Lester family arrived in Madison County.

However, we do know that at least two of the Lesters enjoyed politics.

Alabama originally entered the Union as a state in 1819, with a single at-large House district represented by Gabriel Moore, a prominent lawyer from Huntsville and a leading partisan of the anti-Royalist faction in early state politics. Alabama grew quickly enough between statehood and the reapportionment that followed the 1820 census that, when the census results took full effect in 1823, it had gained two additional seats. Throughout August 1823, the three electoral districts of Alabama elected their newest members to the House of Representatives.

This was during the Era of Good Feelings, a political period lasting from about 1816 to 1824 that overlapped with early Alabama statehood. The War of 1812 had recently ended, reaffirming American independence and leading to the nationwide collapse of the Federalist Party. As a result, the Democratic-Republican Party (an ancestor of the modern Democratic Party) enjoyed unchallenged rule throughout the United States. Those Americans able to vote generally agreed with one another on the federal issues of westward expansion (they wanted more of it), fighting the Natives (a natural consequence of westward expansion) and mail delivery. Thus, elections were more often about intrastate rivalries than national ones.

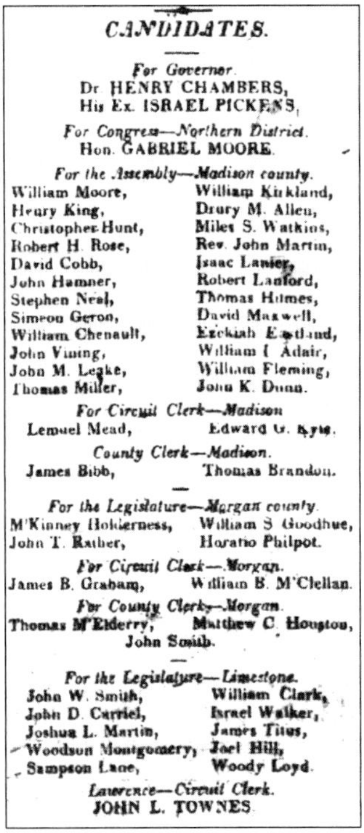

CANDIDATES.

For Governor.
Dr. HENRY CHAMBERS,
His Ex. ISRAEL PICKENS,

For Congress—Northern District.
Hon. GABRIEL MOORE.

For the Assembly—Madison county.

William Moore,	William Kirkland,
Henry King,	Drury M. Allen,
Christopher Hunt,	Miles S. Watkins,
Robert H. Rose,	Rev. John Martin,
David Cobb,	Isaac Lanier,
John Hamner,	Robert Lanford,
Stephen Neal,	Thomas Hilmes,
Simeon Geron,	David Maxwell,
William Chenault,	Ezekiah Eastland,
John Vining,	William I. Adair,
John M. Leake,	William Fleming,
Thomas Miller,	John K. Dunn.

For Circuit Clerk—Madison
Lemuel Mead, Edward G. Kyle.

County Clerk—Madison.
James Bibb, Thomas Brandon.

For the Legislature—Morgan county.
M'Kinney Holderness, William S. Goodhue,
John T. Rather, Horatio Philpot.

For Circuit Clerk—Morgan.
James B. Graham, William B. M'Clellan.

For County Clerk—Morgan.
Thomas M'Elderry, Matthew C. Houston,
John Smith.

For the Legislature—Limestone.

John W. Smith,	William Clark,
John D. Carriel,	Israel Walker,
Joshua L. Martin,	James Titus,
Woodson Montgomery,	Joel Hill,
Sampson Lane,	Woody Loyd.

Lawrence—Circuit Clerk.
JOHN L. TOWNES.

Candidates for 1823 elections. *Courtesy of the Madison County Special Collections.*

However, early nineteenth-century elections still offered voters the opportunity to socialize with other men. This communality—alongside the cakes, meat and beer that political parties often served to supporters to entice them to the polls—attracted 1,823 Madison County voters to the uncontested reelection of Gabriel Moore on August 4, 1823.[44]

Amid the backdrop of all this national hullabaloo, a terrible crime occurred.

The details are scarce. The court does not list the exact relations among Anne, Edmond, Andrew and Winbush Lester. They all lived in Madison County around the same time, had the same last name and visited one another's homes, and the men lied to protect one another. From there, we can only speculate.

Andrew Lester and Winbush Lester visited the house of Edmond Lester, where Anne Lester already resided, so it appears she was either an older unmarried sister who lived with her brother Edmond or, most likely, his wife. The relationship of Edmond, Andrew and Winbush is unclear. They may have been brothers or a father and two sons. Additionally, they appeared on no tax lists during the era of the Mississippi Territory and on no Alabama state censuses thereafter.

Thus, once again, we have only their brief and heinous local records as proof of their existence.

On August 4, 1823, Edmond attacked Anne. It was a vicious assault. Edmond Lester "did strike beat and kick" her repeatedly on "the head breast belly side and other parts of the body." She writhed in agony as he picked her up to "cast and throw…[her] down unto the ground with great force and violence." Edmond did this again. And again. And again, until Anne succumbed to the "several mortal strokes wounds and bruises" she sustained from his savagery. Edmond dragged her body to the Flint River. He looked on this bountiful waterway that fed so much cropland and connected the interior of Madison County to the markets of the Tennessee River Valley and decided to "secretly and maliciously…cast to conceal the said Anne Lester so murdered."

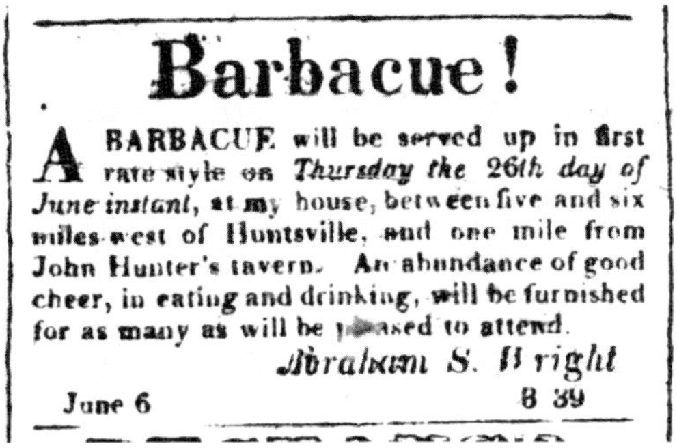

Barbacue!

A BARBACUE will be served up in first rate style on *Thursday the 26th day of June instant*, at my house, between five and six miles west of Huntsville, and one mile from John Hunter's tavern. An abundance of good cheer, in eating and drinking, will be furnished for as many as will be pleased to attend.

Abraham S. Wright

June 6 — 8 39

Above: Political barbecue notice. *Courtesy of the Madison County Special Collections.*

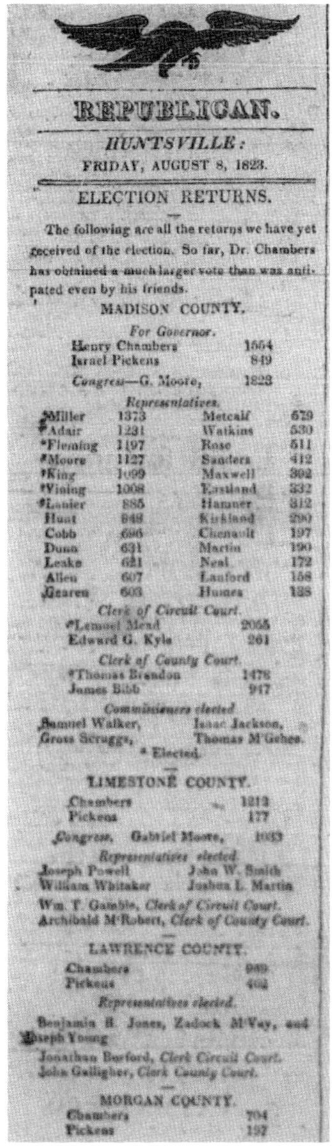

REPUBLICAN.

HUNTSVILLE:

FRIDAY, AUGUST 8, 1823.

ELECTION RETURNS.

The following are all the returns we have yet received of the election. So far, Dr. Chambers has obtained a much larger vote than was antipated even by his friends.

MADISON COUNTY.

For Governor.

Henry Chambers	1664
Israel Pickens	849
Congress—G. Moore,	1823

Representatives.

*Miller	1373	Metcalf	679
*Adair	1231	Watkins	530
*Fleming	1197	Rose	511
*Moore	1127	Sanders	412
*King	1099	Maxwell	392
*Vining	1068	Eastland	332
*Lanier	885	Hanner	312
Hunt	848	Kirkland	290
Cobb	696	Chenault	197
Dunn	631	Martin	190
Leake	621	Neal	172
Allen	607	Lanford	158
Gearen	603	Humes	138

Clerk of Circuit Court.

*Lemuel Mead	2065
Edward G. Kyle	261

Clerk of County Court.

*Thomas Brandon	1478
James Bibb	917

Commissioners elected.

Samuel Walker, Isaac Jackson,
Gross Scruggs, Thomas M'Gehee.

* Elected.

LIMESTONE COUNTY.

Chambers	1213
Pickens	177
Congress, Gabriel Moore,	1033

Representatives elected.

Joseph Powell, John W. Smith
William Whitaker, Joshua L. Martin

Wm. T. Gamble, *Clerk of Circuit Court.*
Archibald M'Robert, *Clerk of County Court.*

LAWRENCE COUNTY.

Chambers	969
Pickens	402

Representatives elected.

Benjamin B. Jones, Zadock M'Vay, and Joseph Young

Jonathan Burford, *Clerk Circuit Court.*
John Galligher, *Clerk County Court.*

MORGAN COUNTY.

Chambers	704
Pickens	197

Right: 1823 election results. *Courtesy of the Madison County Special Collections.*

It did not take long to find her body. From the bruises and lacerations that covered the corpse, including "one mortal wound on the left side of the head…of the length of one inch and of the depth of one inch and one mortal bruise on the back…of the length of six inches and of the breadth of six inches," it took even less time to figure out she didn't drown.

The Lesters closed ranks around Edmond. He couldn't have committed the crime, they claimed, because they had "returned to the house of said Edmond in said county at or about one or two oclock PM of that day." They attempted to provide an alibi for their relation.

But there had been an election, and they liked politics. Madison County possessed only a handful of polling places. For the 1824 presidential election, only the courthouse, "Hazlegreen, Hillsborough, Griffins, Brazletons (in the Big Cove), Ditto's Landing, Triana, Farley's (Lewis old place), Leonard's and Meridianville" served as polling locations. On August 4, 1823, people voted. More than a few recognized Andrew and Winbush Lester and told the sheriff that they "did not leave…but on the contrary thereof remained at the place of election to wit Griffins until the going down of the sun of that day."[45]

Edmond Lester had no alibi because his relatives refused to leave all the drama of an uncontested election. A jury found both Andrew and Winbush guilty of perjury for their feeble attempt to out-bluff eighteen hundred people. They convicted Edmond Lester of murder, and the judge, Clement C. Clay, decreed that he should spend the whole afternoon of the first Friday in January 1824 "between the hours of twelve and three oclock" waiting anxiously as the sheriff readied him to be hanged.

The Merits of Burket Green

Daniel Rather appeared before the Madison County Circuit Court in May 1823. By all accounts, it was a typical case: Judge Clement C. Clay presided, Solicitor Joseph Eastland laid out the facts against Rather and Thomas McCrary served as admirably as one could as a foreman of the grand jury. They considered the weight of Rather's crime, and it was not especially light. He had been negligent in the extreme, and it put others at risk.

He served as a constable, more specifically as "keeper of the…Gaol" in Huntsville. Prisoners often resided there for short stints, because the most violent and egregious crimes ended with more immediate punishments, like being put in the public stocks, branding or long drops from a short rope. Thus, most prisoners served their time uneventfully, escapes occurred maybe once or twice a year and Daniel Rather usually stayed out of court and posted a notice of the escape in the *Alabama Republican*. However, Rather soon entered the court record books because, in 1823, he dealt with a prisoner unlike many of the others he had detained. On April 10, 1823, he "unlawfully and negligently did permit the said Burket Green…to escape and go at Large… whithsoever he would to the great hindrance and obstruction of Justice in contempt of the laws of the said State of Alabama."

Burket Green, this man whom Daniel Rather failed to keep in jail, is first described in the court records by his occupation: he was a yeoman, a small-hold farmer. For a brief moment, Green existed as another iteration of the Jeffersonian ideal. However, the documents soon take a disturbing turn as we learn that the circuit court considered him a man "moved and seduced by the Instigation of the Devil."

On April 29, 1821, Green attacked a man named Warren Hart. It was a Sunday, thus a day during which people rarely traveled. The records described both men as being residents of Madison County at the time of the

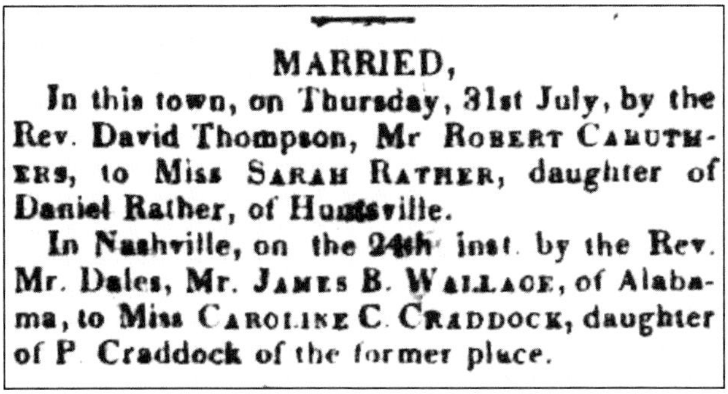

MARRIED,

In this town, on Thursday, 31st July, by the Rev. David Thompson, Mr ROBERT CARUTHERS, to Miss SARAH RATHER, daughter of Daniel Rather, of Huntsville.

In Nashville, on the 24th inst. by the Rev. Mr. Dales, Mr. JAMES B. WALLACE, of Alabama, to Miss CAROLINE C. CRADDOCK, daughter of P. Craddock of the former place.

Rather wedding notice. *Courtesy of the Madison County Special Collections.*

assault. Their joint descriptions as yeomen and inhabitants of the county and the timing of the assault all indicate that they knew each other and lived near each other.

Unfortunately, communal bonds frayed enough that when Green and Hart came to blows, Burket Green fell upon his opponent like a demon. Green grabbed Hart "with both his hands" and pummeled his head relentlessly, eventually focusing his anger on an area "behind the right ear" of Warren Hart. With fury and "malice aforethought," Green pounded the back of Hart's head until his fists sunk into the other man's skull—leaving an indentation two inches wide and two inches deep.

Not content to simply crack another man's skull, Green continued his assault. He grabbed Hart and "did beat and throw [him] down to the floor." While Hart lay prone, bleeding and injured, Green took it upon himself to "strike and kick" Hart's "head neck breast Belly sides and back," until he was bleeding and covered in bruises.

Then came the killing blow.

After this vicious assault, Burket Green did not turn away from Warren Hart and leave him to writhe in agony on the ground. No, Green saw the soft and vulnerable target presented by Hart's exposed belly.

He lifted his right foot and "did Beat Bruise and Stamp on the lower part" of Hart's stomach. Green slammed his foot into the soft tissues around Hart's colon and small intestines with such violence that it left deep and awful bruises "of the length of six inches and of the breadth of four inches."

Warren Hart survived the initial onslaught but suffered as he slowly shuffled off his mortal coil. After four days of agonizing pain, Hart succumbed to "the striking bruising beating and kicking aforesaid [and] died."

Although he had clearly killed a man in a brutal way, the jury proved itself lenient in the case of Burket Green and, on November 26, 1822, found him "not Guilty of murder as charged in said Indictment." It considered the fact that Warren Hart's death resulted from a prolonged fit of animalistic rage and lacked prior planning or motivation. In a roundabout way, Green's cruel and immediate conduct may have saved him. The jury settled on the lesser charge of manslaughter and ruled his "term of Imprisonment to be twelve months and…his fine to be five hundred dollars." A letter from the local solicitor, Joseph Eastland, to Governor Israel Pickens emphatically dated July 3, 1823, states that Eastland "considerably [thought] Green merits death" for his crimes. Not content with his good fortune in avoiding the noose, on April 10, 1823, Green overpowered Daniel Rather in the city jail and absconded "before the twelve months was expired."[46]

He did not long enjoy freedom. Less than a month later, on May 5, 1823, Green appeared before the court to answer for his attempted escape. The jury took his case to heart a second time. Instead of heaping more prison time on this man who cared little for the laws of Alabama or the confines of its prisons, it found "the defendant not Guilty of breaking the Jail but Guilty of a misdemeanor and assess his fine to Fifty Dollars."

As for Daniel Rather, though he allowed the escape of a violent and dangerous man, the jury ultimately found him not guilty. It reviewed all the actions of his charge and agreed that there existed extenuating circumstances. After all, who could be expected to contain such a man as Burket Green?

SHOULD BE IN HELL OR TEXAS

On April 20, 1846, Thomas M. Marley walked with Philip Pritchett for a while. They headed west toward Limestone County and the jail where Marley intended to temporarily detain Pritchett "for safe keeping." Thomas Marley was the sheriff of Madison County, and people told him that they had seen Philip Pritchett shoot a man that morning. So now, with Pritchett in custody and little said between them, they walked.

Pritchett eventually broke the silence. He turned to the sheriff and said "that he had killed Stammers & was sorry for it—but that he thought he had done it to save his own life." Pritchett told the sheriff everything. He was not afraid of Henry Stammers but of two other men. Edward Lewis and Aaron McGaha had come to him and said that if he did not kill Stammers, they would kill him. Above all, Pritchett regretted not taking his wife's advice. If he had, "he never would have done the deed."

April 15, 1846

According to Jarvis H. Poor, the two men argued over the stabling fees for a horse. Poor was a justice of the peace and, five days before the murder, had issued a warrant "for an open amount" against Henry Stammers in Pritchett's favor. Jarvis Poor had heard the arguments from both men and found Philip Pritchett's claims for compensation for keeping Stammers's horse more convincing. Henry Stammers insisted that the only way forward was if Pritchett "would give up the Horse…& charge nothing for board." If Pritchett let the matter go, Stammers would as well. Henry Stammers returned to see Jarvis Poor three more times. Twice he told Poor that if Pritchett did not agree to his terms, then "one or the other should be in hell or Texas before the warrant executed."

Jarvis Poor pleaded with Henry Stammers to reconsider such bold and ready words. He reminded Stammers to consider the consequences of his actions "and warned him to think of Judgement death & Divinity."

Stammers confided to Poor that he had attempted to buy a gun but that nobody would sell one to him because they knew he intended to murder Philip Pritchett with it. Ignoring Poor's earlier remonstrations that

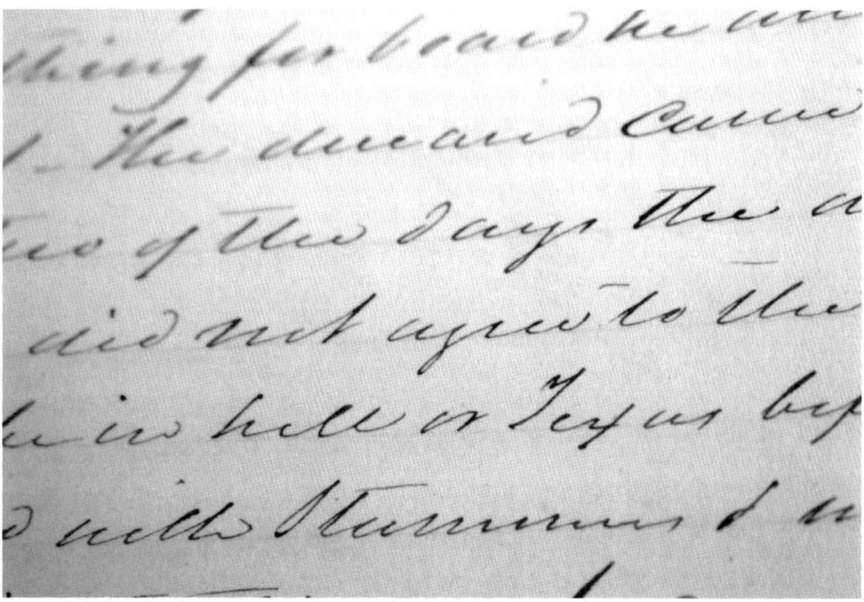

Hell or Texas. *Courtesy of the Madison County Probate Archives.*

murder might be harmful to the soul, Stammers told him he would get a gun, even "if he had to go into some man's home & take it by force." Poor told Pritchett about Henry Stammers's demands and odd threats about Texas. No one else knew of the problems between them.

April 19, 1846

Joseph Elliott worked his fields. A voice called for him from the road. Philip Pritchett beckoned him over, but Elliott called back and said he could not, as he was working. Pritchett demanded to speak to Elliott, so he came to meet him in the fields. Pritchett spoke lividly and told Elliott that if Henry Stammers came "within forty yards of him that he would kill him." He described what had transpired that morning. Earlier, when Pritchett went to tend his fields, "Stammers with a pistol in one hand & a stick or rock in the other" menaced Pritchett on his way to his plough. He said that Stammers had made threats against him. Joseph Elliott never heard of any such threats, and after Pritchett left, he went on with his work.

The Morning of the Killing

According to witnesses and court records, the horror started early that day.

John Webb walked past Pritchett's home, "which was immediately on the roadside." He noticed Philip Pritchett emerge with a rifle, "which he was priming or picking & was then trying."

June MacHee, an eleven-year-old girl, walked to school along the road that ran next to Henry Stammers's home. She heard a loud angry voice, which she recognized as Pritchett's, call out, "Stop I have come to shoot you!" June watched as Stammers turned around. She kept walking.

The gunfire echoed across the valley.

June MacHee saw Henry Stammers fall and watched as Philip Pritchett ran away. When she got to school, she informed her teacher of the crime. Testifying six years later, she made sure to comment on how the murder impacted her, and she said that she still had "a distinct recollection of these facts."

When Joseph Elliott "heard the report of a rifle" he immediately started out toward the home of Henry Stammers. On his way there, he came across Pritchett "in a trot or rapid walk looking back frequently." He found

Henry Stammers "shot open…near his house on his own land," already dead from his wounds.

Philip Pritchett waited longer for his murder trial to start than did most other defendants of the time. It dragged on for five years before he was indicted. The crime was so obvious and infamous that the sheriff after Marley, C.D. Kavanaugh, could not find enough impartial jurors in Huntsville to form a grand jury. The first three years of the trial focused on getting Philip Pritchett in court. From 1846 to 1849, the court issued multiple writs of alias capias—the official summons issued when someone misses a court date prior to their plea. Eventually, constables found Pritchett and detained him in the Madison County Jail.

Jurors deliberated over his fate; their discussions dragged on so long that the court spent $60 putting them all up in the Bell Tavern. In September 1849, the jurors came forth and said "they cannot agree" for which crime he should be charged. Pritchett briefly tasted freedom on a $4,000 bond but must have tried to evade another court summons, because afterward, he never appeared before the court without shackles on again.

Finally, during the August and September term of the court in 1852, a jury agreed. Philip Pritchett was found guilty of murder in the second degree. Jurors sentenced him to "be conveyed from hence with all correct despatch to the state Penitentiary at Wetumpka, there to be confined for the period of ten years."[47]

If only he had listened to his wife.

3
HATE CRIMES

Introduction

Enslaved humans in the Mississippi Territory and Alabama supposedly possessed legal rights. The framers of the 1807 *Statutes of the Mississippi Territory* wished to "protect this useful, but degraded class of men, from cruelty and oppression" by outlawing cruel and unusual punishments. In 1817, Alabama and Mississippi adopted nearly identical constitutional provisions dealing with enslaved humans. Mississippi allowed enslaved people to stand trial only when they were accused of murder and had no minimum sentencing requirements for when white people assaulted and murdered them.

In Alabama, enslaved people were legally guaranteed trials for any crime above petty larceny. The law claimed that local courts would prosecute their dismemberment or murder as if "the like offence had been committed on a free white person." Legally, the enslaved people of Alabama possessed the most basic protections for life and limb, and when they were accused of crimes, they would see their day in court.[48]

Laws mean nothing when nobody enforces them.

Throughout the territorial period and into early statehood, assaults on the enslaved population by White men were common. The assaults usually occurred on Wednesday and Saturday afternoons and on Sundays. Local markets ran until noon on Wednesdays and Saturdays, while people

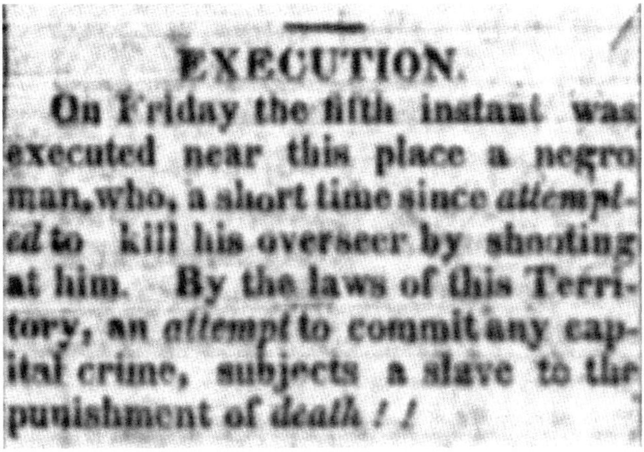

EXECUTION.

On Friday the fifth instant was executed near this place a negro man, who, a short time since *attempted* to kill his overseer by shooting at him. By the laws of this Territory, an *attempt* to commit any capital crime, subjects a slave to the punishment of *death!!*

Execution. *Courtesy of the Madison County Special Collections.*

attended church services and visited relatives on Sunday. These assaults clustered around times of activity, commerce and leisure. Most assaults occurred in public and involved large groups of White men.

The suits were rarely prosecuted on behalf of the enslaved people but instead consisted of suits for damages between White men. Court records indicate that when enslaved people were accused of crimes, their trials were omitted from the official record, appearing as literal blank pages in the court books or, like the above 1819 announcement of the execution of an enslaved man for shooting at an overseer, mentioned briefly in the local paper with no recorded trial.

Which is why this section is separate from other murders and assaults. Enslaved people received only the most token of legal protections in antebellum Alabama, and the laws bestowing rights upon enslaved people were inherently contradictory. Property cannot have rights, and a human cannot be owned. The slave system's chief export was brutality. The normalization of violence and dehumanization of enslaved people meant that nearby mobs of white people felt justified in attacking, demeaning and murdering them. Every effort has been made to make the victims the centerpiece of each case examined. It is a challenging task due to the paucity of records. Hopefully, this section bestows on the reader a fuller understanding of the constant dangers of the life of enslaved people in Alabama, an experience in which the law was often absent and every white person a potential assailant.

The Starvation of Dennis

Dennis was an enslaved youth in the Mississippi Territory. Court records described him as "a negro boy slave…the property of Douglas I. Puckel." Sadly, no other records of him exist beyond a few lines in this court case. The circuit court's willingness to refer to him as a "boy slave" establishes he is young but is otherwise ambivalent. Children and young adults who appeared in circuit court records were referred to as infants, girls or boys prior to attaining the age of majority at twenty-one. Other cases involving enslaved youths or white children demonstrate differences in usage; in separate incidences, the court referred to an enslaved teenager as a girl and to a nineteen-year-old white man as an infant. The reference point of "boy" establishes that Dennis was old enough to work but younger than twenty-one.

Douglas Puckel never appeared on the 1809 Squatter Census nor on any Madison County tax lists and probably only spent a brief period of time in the area.

In August 1811, Puckel rented Dennis out to a man named John Bell, so the boy was "then and there in his possession and…protection." Bell, like the other two people named in the case, was absent on later tax lists and appeared in no further court records, which described Bell as a laborer and little else.

They did, however, take note of his crimes. On August 25, 1811, John Bell "evilly and cruelly entreated" Dennis, beating the youth so much that he did "drive away" the boy, who was "forced to flee into the woods…near the house of John Bell." Dennis resided in the protection of the forest for several days, but the "beating brusing wounding and evil and cruel treatment" of John Bell, coupled with the "hunger and thirst" he experienced, led to his death on September 1, 1811. The jurors looked on John Bell as a murderer, easily concluding that his actions resulted in Dennis being "kill[ed], murder[ed], and starved."

However, the court did not convene until "the first Monday in October 1811," which allowed Bell enough time to either leave or make friends. The grand jurors returned a "no true bill," which meant that the crime would not be prosecuted, either due to Bell's absence or to a lack of evidence to convince an all-white jury that Dennis was starved to death by John Bell's hand.

Nobody ever prosecuted John Bell for murder.[49]

The Murder of Daniel

Daniel died on a Wednesday. His only description in the court records is as a "negro man slave" owned by one William Leslie. He was probably over the age of twenty-one and had resided in Madison County for at least a year by the time of his death.

One must describe the world and people around him. Court documents described William Leslie as a planter, an uncommon description for 1813. Leslie focused on amassing humans over acreage. Although his total owned land remained static at 160 acres for much of the 1810s, the number of people he enslaved increased steadily, with fourteen slaves in 1812 and an additional two in 1813. Even though a smattering of other men in Huntsville owned two or three times as many people as Leslie, he is one of the few planters ever described by the court. This might indicate that, although his landholdings remained comparable to most yeomen, his acreage was under intensive forced cultivation. Or he simply held more slaves than the average participant in a circuit court case, and the court clerk felt the need to differentiate.[50]

On a Wednesday in April, Daniel ran afoul of a man named Randolph Rogers. Rogers appeared only on the 1812 Tax List. He owned no acreage but held two slaves, whom he probably rented out to others. The court described him as a laborer, so he toiled for others, and two enslaved people toiled for him.[51]

There is no evidence for the reasoning behind their quarrel. On April 14, 1813, Rogers brandished "a certain rifle gun made of iron" at Daniel before firing at him. The bullet hurled forward by "force of gunpowder" and struck Daniel "a little below the left pap" or nipple. It tore through him, leaving behind a "mortal wound of the depth of six inches and of the breadth of one inch" from which he instantly died.

The jurors found Rogers not guilty of murder, sentencing him to the lesser charge of manslaughter. Jurors balked at the prospect of potentially hanging a white man over the death of an enslaved human. Instead, they had Rogers "immediately branded in open court on the left hand with the letter M." Branding was an uncommon punishment in Madison County and usually reserved for thieves. This, more than any other punishment, probably impacted Rogers the most. The jury also demanded a $500 fine and six months in prison and decreed that on July 12, 1813, he should stand for "two hours in the pillory." It is unclear if Rogers ever paid the fine. He quickly disappeared from Madison County's tax lists after 1812 and likely fled to escape the shame of what he did.[52]

But, ultimately, Randolph Rogers still got to live, a luxury he had denied to Daniel on a Wednesday in April 1813.

ASSAULT ON LUCKEY

On Sunday, June 3, 1821, James E. Smith committed a terrible crime. Court records described Smith as a yeoman, or a small landowner. Smith lived in Madison County only briefly. He failed to appear on any of the Mississippi Territory Tax Lists and disappeared from later censuses and court records. It is likely that Smith arrived between 1815 and 1821.

On that June 3, a young girl named Luckey, who was "under the age of ten years to wit of the age of eight years," unknowingly embodied the cognitive dissonance of the slave system. Described briefly as a "a female slave of colour the property of William Dillard," she possessed few rights in nineteenth-century Alabama.

Luckey's encounter with James E. Smith immediately reminded the people of Madison County of her undoubtable humanity. Smith attacked Luckey, violently beating her before he "wound cut and ill treat" her so badly that people thought she might die. Smith originally intended to "ravish and casually known and abase" the eight-year-old girl. She fought back against the devil named James E. Smith. Her resistance bought her time and prevented Smith's "attempt to commit a rape" but cost her blood and broken bones.

William Dillard, upset at Luckey's lost productivity, filed charges against Smith. The case came before the court on September 3, 1821, and was presided over by prominent men. Jurors included Samuel Cruse, Henry Bibb and Ezekiel Madkins, who were, respectively, a local lawyer, a member of the political dynasty that produced Alabama's first two governors and a long-settled plantation owner in western Madison County. The group, regardless of individual prestige, made short work of the case. They quickly found James E. Smith guilty and fined him "twenty Dollars" for his viciousness and evil.

Smith's lawyers immediately petitioned the court to show "why a new trial shall not be had in this case" and convinced the judge of unspecified procedural errors. The judge understood that Smith might have legal standing but planned to imprison him until the next term of the court to prevent his flight.

Terms of the court usually occurred every six months, with an April and September term punctuated by the occasional special session. Smith proved unwilling to wait in the county jail until April 1822 and summoned associates to give a bond for that September term. George Smith, David Royster and William Kirkland all agreed to pay "three hundred and thirty three dollars each" in addition to a secondary $1,000 bond given by James E. Smith himself. The court allowed James E. Smith to go free and counted on the dual pressures of financial ruin and community policing to ensure that he appeared at the next term of the court.

On April 29, 1822, James E. Smith petitioned to be "discharged from further appearance." This means he may have simply paid the twenty dollars to William Dillard, but it precluded the further justice of the court. Smith left without the slightest legal burden.

Luckey's case was extraordinary not for the gross miscarriage of justice that was its outcome, but because it existed at all. Enslaved people were routinely attacked by whites from all levels of the social strata. However, I have found no other cases from antebellum Madison County that explicitly mentioned rape or described a sexual assault. It would be ludicrous to think that James E. Smith was the only rapist in the county or that other assaults on women in the local court records were not the result of resistance to sexual assault.

An eight-year-old enslaved girl was the only plaintiff to accuse her attacker of the crimes he committed and demand justice for the damage he had done. The immediacy with which the jury found James Smith guilty spoke to the brutality and horror of the assault, and the immediacy with which the court found a loophole for a well-connected white man was a terrible reminder of the distribution of power in the Old South.[53]

The Great Terror of Tom and Milly

September 15, 1822, was a Sunday. Rather than spend the day in quiet reflection, Anderson Wisson, Francis L. Adams and Littleberry Wade, along with an unnamed group of men "to the number of ten or more," chose to "riotously routously and tumultuously" rampage through the streets of Huntsville. For six hours they roamed the city, a crowd of at least thirteen men "making such noises" and causing "great terror" to the inhabitants of the city.

Their presence disrupted traffic as the rowdy mass disturbed travelers along the "public streets Huses and common highways" of Huntsville. They carried weapons and used them to threaten passersby. No constable approached to stop them, nor did the sheriff see fit to disperse the horde. These men prowled the streets unmolested by the law and unencumbered of decency.

Then they came upon Tom and Milly, both of whom the court records briefly describe as "a negro slave." There are no further descriptions of either of them, not even a brief mention of their age. Their whole presence is three words long.

There is no clear indication if the mob caught Tom or Milly first, or if they assaulted both of them simultaneously, because the court described both assaults with rote language. What is clear is that one of the men, likely Littleberry Wade, produced "a certain club." The group of men "grievously cut bruised and wounded" Tom and Milly, striking them hard enough with the club to bring forth blood.

Their injuries indicate that Tom and Milly curled up to try to protect themselves from the brutal assault. They sustained terrible bruises on their "head arms sides back and other parts" of their bodies. The court recorded that the group of men possessed a burning desire to "kill and murder" both of the enslaved people with their onslaught of "terrible grievous and dangerous Blows." Miraculously, they survived.[54]

Charges were brought against three men. The court met as regularly scheduled on May 5, 1823, yet something unlikely occurred. For the first time in Madison County's legal history, no mention was made of Tom or Milly's owners, nor was anyone besides Joseph Eastland, the solicitor for the circuit court, listed as a prosecutor. The injustice done to Tom and Milly was severe enough that the local courts decided to pursue a case "in behalf of the State."

A similar pair of cases from the following year illustrates the strangeness of Tom and Milly's appearance in the court records. On July 19, 1823, Williamson Land assaulted two enslaved men, Stephen and Dempsey, who were owned by Richard Holden and Davis Battles, respectively. In each case, the court described the attacks and claimed that Williamson Land nearly took both of the enslaved men's lives. Land appeared before the circuit court on November 3, 1823. However, when listing the damages done by Land, the circuit court wrote that he "did other wrongs to the said Stephen…to the great damage of said Richard," and while it was true he nearly killed Dempsey, he actually caused the "great damage of Davis Battles."

It might not immediately appear as one of the rarest of moments, but the usage of "to the great damage of the said Tom and…the said Milly" marked the only instance when the circuit court prosecuted an assault on an enslaved person without a slaveholder as the prosecutor.

Jurors found Francis L. Adams guilty only of rioting and issued him a twenty-five-dollar fine. Anderson Wisson and Littleberry Wade escaped the first two charges—rioting and beating Tom—but found themselves judged responsible for the attack on Milly. Wisson was fined ten dollars. Littleberry Wade might have instigated the attack or been the most brutal, because the jury fined him fifty dollars and ordered that he be kept "in custody of the Sheriff" until he managed to pay.

One can only hope it took a while for him to secure the funds.

4
LIQUOR, KIDNAPPING AND PROSTITUTION

Much Hilarity, Great Noise and Disturbance

Huntsville buzzed with anticipation throughout the summer of 1819. The short-lived Alabama Territory stood poised to become a state. The Adams-Onís Treaty had been signed in February, and it ceded not just the long-sought West Florida to the United States but East Florida as well. All of South America seemed to be overflowing with revolutionary fervor, and the exploits of Simón Bolívar against the Spanish empire dominated the local paper. Most amazingly, on June 1, President James Monroe briefly visited the young town, meeting with notable locals before retiring to a large banquet at around four o'clock in the afternoon. It was a heady time on the rapidly closing southwestern frontier.

Leaders of the local militia, merchants and land speculators toasted the president, the Constitution and "the memories of those who fell" in the War of 1812. Then, Monroe rose and responded with toasts of his own. He knew his audience and drank not only to the health of Andrew Jackson but also mentioned local hero John Coffee's nighttime raid on the British headquarters at Villeré Plantation, stating, "as long as we remember the 8th January, we cannot forget the 23d Dec'r." Cannons roared as he spoke.

The feast ended around sunset, and President Monroe's rustic affectations had transformed him in the local imagination from the "Chief Magistrate of a great nation" to a plain-spoken first among equals. He departed

Huntsville on June 3, 1819, with many of the "respectable citizens" of the county trailing after the president on the road to Nashville as he rode off into the sunrise.[55]

Scarcely a month later, the constitutional convention began. The people of Madison County had high hopes for the founding document of their new state. The *Alabama Republican* opined that the convention stood to benefit from the combined wisdom of the "most enlightened late citizens" of Georgia, Virginia and the Carolinas. Citizens wrote to the paper with hopeful suggestions for the delegates: one wanted Alabama to have a small council instead of a single governor; another wished for the new state to be renamed Washington; a third petitioned the convention that "slavery may be abolished by a provision" in the new constitution. The future seemed bright.[56]

The convention was set to meet for the first time on Monday, July 5, 1819. Out of respect for the Sabbath, the Fourth of July celebrations were moved to Saturday, so delegates gathered at the Huntsville Inn on July 3 and once again toasted the U.S. Constitution, the young country and its growing number of war dead. They sang the praises of Andrew Jackson, quoting Duke Vincentio from Shakespeare's *Measure for Measure* to describe their love for him: "The whitest virtue strikes." Someone proclaimed their desire for the newly acquired West Florida to become part of Alabama. Then John Taylor stood up and read the Declaration of Independence. The delegates and other notable citizens dispersed around 3:00 p.m. with "much hilarity, and without any disturbance or accident."[57]

Amid the merriment, expectations about the social structure of this new state temporarily frayed. Although the delegates included judges, congressmen, lawyers and merchants, they brought with them ropemakers, sawyers, cowboys, farmers and cooks—people who exemplified as much of the distilled genius of Virginia, Georgia and the Carolinas as the "most enlightened late citizens" who held feasts, met with the president and wrote editorials in the *Alabama Republican*. Yet, the second group came in chains.

The enslaved population of Huntsville understood that excitement ran across the landscape. They knew a presidential visit and rounds of feasting were abnormal. They understood that Alabama was about to enter the nation as a full member.

So, when July 4, 1819, arrived, it was a perfect storm of jovial opportunity. Not only was it a holiday, but it also took place on a Sunday. Not every enslaved person would have had Sundays to themselves, but the Sabbath was traditionally associated with an amount of leisure time for enslaved people, and it was common throughout Virginia and the Carolinas for slaveholders to allow this solitary day of rest. So, a major holiday happened on the only day of the week that enslaved people got to themselves, while the whole territory rested on the cusp of statehood. It was an exciting time to be in the city.

When one is in an exciting time and place, it is common to go looking for a drink. On Sunday, July 4, 1819, members of the enslaved population of Huntsville did exactly that. They found a series of white men more than willing to sell them alcohol. Daniel Murphy, the brothers James Badlem and William Badlem, James Black and Woody Martin were all listed in their separate cases as grocers. They probably owned stalls they set up on market days and ran stores from their own homes throughout the rest of the week. Unlike larger merchants, they did not frequently post ads in the newspaper. They gained their business by word of mouth.

Court documents described each man as operating an "ill governed and disorderly house" where, throughout the summer of 1819, on "divers other days being Sabbath days" they routinely sold "spiritous Liquors to negro slaves." Either authorities chose to ignore the previous instances of Sunday drinking or the buyers were few enough in number to avoid attention. However, on this Fourth of July, the enslaved, along with "persons of evil name fame and dishonest conversation," came out in large enough numbers to make a "great noise and disturbance," which alerted the law to their presence.[58]

Local elites balked at the prospect of Whites, free Blacks and enslaved people spending any recreational time together. In August 1821, a common laborer named Giles G. Boggs received a fifty-dollar fine because he and an enslaved man named Peter played "a game with cards for money." If a game of cards alerted the law, then selling liquor to large groups of enslaved people quickly drew the court's attention. Murphy, Black, Martin and the Badlem brothers first came before the court on October 4, 1819. However, the docket proved too large for them to be tried that term, and Henry Minor, attorney general for the Northern District of the Alabama Territory, rescheduled each man to reappear before the court on March 6, 1820.[59]

Time and again, if a defendant found their trial delayed, their likelihood of evading punishment increased exponentially. In March 1820, one after the other, Woody Martin, James Black and William and James Badlem learned that the indictment and evidence against them proved "defective and insufficient" and that they got to go home. Daniel Murphy got a $200 fine.

Most of the men never reappeared in court, and for years, few grocers risked the fate of Daniel Murphy by selling alcohol to enslaved people. However, Woody Martin reemerged in the court record in 1823. He had spent the previous year and the first months of 1823 illegally operating an unlicensed "house of Entertainment for travelers," where he not only allowed the road weary to stop and rest but also sold them "corn fodder Meat and Bread" and liquor. He appeared before the court on May 5, 1823. Shockingly, Martin decided to sell a half pint of whiskey to a lawyer named Nimrod Fielder on the way to the courthouse and, on his arrival for his original infraction, was faced with a second case. Jurors issued Martin a twenty-dollar fine for brazenly offloading illegal whiskey on his court date and consigned him to the local jail until he paid.[60]

On September 1, 1823, Philip Hoffman sold a variety of liquors and "fermented drinks" to the enslaved people "of sundry of the good citizens" of Huntsville. They assembled at his home, which also hosted his shop, where he encouraged them to "tipple drink [and] carouse" loudly for several hours on a Monday. This immediate threat to the "good order economy and safety" of Huntsville attracted the law's attention, and constables soon arrived to shut it down.

Hoffman remained unperturbed; the constables remained vigilant. On the next day, September 2, Hoffman was caught selling unlicensed whiskey and brandy to a trio of white men named Richard Clemens, Henry Webb and John Cox. Constables found him attempting to retail spirits to the same three men again a month later.

When Philip Hoffman came before the court on November 3, 1823, he tried a novel tactic. He chose not to plead not guilty and hope to get his trial delayed long enough for the state to drop his cases. Hoffman pleaded guilty to all three charges and put himself upon "the grace and mercy of the court." Surprisingly, it worked. Rather than punish him to the same extent as Daniel Murphy in 1819, or even Woody Martin, who had faced a relatively steep fine a few months prior, the court issued him a series of symbolic fines: one dollar for selling liquor to the enslaved, five dollars for the first attempt to sell liquor to the three white men and another dollar for his second one.[61]

White men often sold each other unlicensed alcohol with few lasting repercussions. For decades, the illegal distribution of whiskey and other liquors remained the most common reason for a person to appear before the court. Men also appeared before the court for gambling as often as for selling spirits without a license. Every class of white man sold unlicensed liquor to one another and either hosted or played at illegal faro, roulette wheels and billiards tables in one another's homes and hotels. They tippled, drank and caroused at every occasion and generally played cards where they pleased. Even the sheriff, Stephen Neal, found himself on the wrong side of the law when, in 1822, he sold half a pint of whiskey to John Sproul.[62]

Conversely, the grocers, merchants and gamblers who dared sell liquor to the enslaved or play cards with them often met swift justice. Their mercantile activities temporarily ignored the social norms regarding control of the enslaved population and allowed an amount of recreation equal to what a white person might enjoy. The merchants who sold them liquor and the white men who gambled with them certainly did not do so out of any sentiment more progressive than their desire for a dollar. These interactions, however brief, provoked outrage from other white people. Philip Hoffman, who readily admitted to his guilt and pleaded for mercy, seems to be the only exception.

After the early 1820s, mentions of enslaved people purchasing alcohol disappear from court records, and unlike the lack of prosecution for prostitution, there are no other hints of it emerging in civil cases. While enslaved people probably continued to imbibe alcohol, it was most likely homemade, or they traded for it in secret. There would be no more open sales to them. This mirrored other increasing restrictions on slave life as Madison County fully transitioned from a newly opened frontier into a province of the cotton kingdom. Between 1828 and 1831, the city issued a variety of ordinances barring enslaved people from living separately from their owners or selling their own produce in the market. While these later restrictions curbed the privacy and economic autonomy of the enslaved, the handful of cases between 1819 and 1823 and the harsher punishments dealt to the involved merchants showed that the white elite first sought to limit the ability of the enslaved to enjoy the "much hilarity" so cherished by the men who ran the city.

THE SPINSTERS OF MADISON COUNTY

The legislative history of prostitution in Alabama is little more than a scattershot of ink across the centuries. While the state's legislators spilled barrels of ink over their major anxieties like slavery, road construction and gambling, sex workers appeared in the record as a habitual afterthought, tucked away as subsections of other laws, their fates to be decided by a patchwork of municipal ordinances.

The earliest direct mention of the word *prostitute* is from 1819, when the legislature passed an act incorporating the City of Mobile. Section 7 of the law declared it legal for the mayor and aldermen of Mobile to demand security from drunks, the homeless and "public prostitutes" to ensure their continued orderly behavior and self-sufficiency. If they failed to prove their ability to avoid public support, then the mayor and aldermen might periodically round them up and force them to labor "for a limited time"—usually less than four months. These words and enumerated powers appear verbatim in other cities' incorporating legislation.

The next explicit mention of prostitutes or prostitution came from an 1824 act amending an earlier divorce law. It reiterates that if spouses knew of an occurrence of adultery but forgave the offender, then they could not reasonably seek a divorce for it later. Legislators felt the need to add that the "plaintiff (if the husband) allowed of his wife's prostitution, it shall be a bar against divorce."[63]

The legislature remained mostly silent on the issue until 1841. Chapter 3 of "An Act Regulating Punishments under the Penitentiary System" established the mandatory minimum sentences for a variety of crimes; forcing an adult woman to marry you resulted in seven years, and rape was a life sentence. But kidnapping "any female under the age of twelve years" and forcing her to become a concubine or prostitute carried the much lighter sentence of "not less than two years" in prison.[64]

The Mississippi Territory was a frontier colonized at first by pioneer families and then by a stream of young men from the Atlantic Seaboard and Upper South. They often arrived bored and lonely, seeking refuge in the boardinghouses and Native settlements dotting the sunken log roads. The southwestern frontier attracted and contained the desperate mercantilism of the dispossessed.

Few free women were more dispossessed than the local prostitutes. The laws passed to regulate their existence reveal a life bound by the whims of officials they could not elect, husbands they could rarely leave and childhoods destroyed by captors from the bawdyhouses. As such, most evidence of them is bound in local myths—often about the public health and medicine. In Huntsville, there are stories about land for the first hospital being donated by Madam Mollie Teal, and the University of Alabama–Birmingham issued a public health award named after brothel owner and cholera fighter Louise Wooster.

Mollie Teal Mansion. *Courtesy of the Madison County Special Collections.*

However, in Huntsville in the early 1820s, a group of prostitutes ran afoul of the law often enough that one might glean a better understanding of their life and life for women like them during the territorial and early statehood periods. The first record of prostitutes in the city of Huntsville comes from the September term of the 1820 circuit court. Joseph Eastland, the solicitor for the city, charged seven women. He alleged that on January 1, 1820, "and on divers other days and times," they operated a "certain Bawdy house" within city limits.

Alabama officially entered the Union on December 14, 1819, so the new year of 1820 held symbolic significance for the state's inhabitants. They left their brief sojourn as the Alabama Territory and entered fully into nationhood. With all of the intense feelings about statehood, it was inevitable that the new year attracted revelry, but the court describes nothing less than a new Gomorrah.

Rodah Barnett, Mary Baker, Elizabeth Burton, Mary King, Ann Martin, Barbara Wilson and Lucinda Wilson lived in Huntsville and kept a "certain Bawdy house unlawfully and wickedly." The court described them as spinsters, a colloquial term used to describe unmarried women regardless of age. Though it later morphed to become synonymous with an older unmarried woman, during this time, officials might classify a young woman as a spinster more readily than use the legal terminology *feme sole*. Certainly not all spinsters were prostitutes who ran "Bawdy houses," and not all prostitutes were unmarried; but when dealing with this group of women and their court cases in the early 1820s, the traditional moniker for an unwed woman took on a secondary connotation in the language used by the court.[65]

As for their "Bawdy house," the fact that the women "unlawfully" kept it means either all prostitution was banned within the city limits or the women involved failed to purchase licenses for their business. This point is inconclusive because the earliest city council minutes have been lost. Context must provide answers. The county court frequently prosecuted unlicensed taverns. Selling liquor without a license remained one of the most common crimes during the territorial period and early statehood. The city of Huntsville needed revenue, and licensing provided one of its readiest streams of cash. This evidence suggests that the ire directed against these women might have arisen less from moral objections than from the innate desire of bureaucrats to balance their books.

However, Huntsville experienced an influx of reformers focused on public health and morality. These reformers expressed ready interest in the city government, and from the late 1820s onward they introduced a variety of ordinances focused on preventing pollution in the Big Spring, funding public education and an ill-fated attempt at temperance. Contemporary reformist sentiment, combined with the vitriol found in the court's description of the women and their "Bawdy house," points to a banning of prostitution within city limits and their outright flouting of local ordinances.

One can also draw conclusions about the reformers' attitudes toward prostitutes in the aforementioned vitriolic language they used to describe the women and their establishment. They referred to the clients and inhabitants not just as "evil disposed persons" but broke them down into further categories. Inside the "Bawdy house," they found not only men but also "women and whores." By creating a third category separate from either men or women to describe sex workers, the court dis-gendered them and subsequently removed the few social protections afforded to white women in the antebellum period. They were no longer single women but a distinct class all their own.

This other class of women disturbed the social order. The descriptions of the ruckus they raised required far more synonyms than crimes of similar magnitude. When all seven of the women being prosecuted assembled under one roof to commit their "whoredom and fornication," one might be sure that "unlawful assemblies, riots, Routs, affairs, disturbances, and violations of the peace…and dreadful, filthy, and lewd offences" would soon follow. The court painted a picture of absolute pandemonium following in their wake. In a Socratic twist, their mere existence was nothing less than the "manifest distraction ruination and subversion of youth."

David Davis also operated a "common ill governed and disorderly house" during this period. The circuit court asserted that on August 1, 1821, he allowed a variety of people "there to be and remain tippling whoreing and misbehaving themselves." More shockingly, Davis operated a brothel that not only operated on the Sabbath but also served an interracial clientele. Whites and "negroes of ill name and fame and of dishonest conversation" mingled with one another at all hours of the night and day. Despite allowing behavior that undermined and attacked the caste system, no solicitor ever accused Davis of subverting the youth. More tellingly, in every instance in which the court prosecuted women for sex work, it accused them of working "for filthy Lucer." The court clerk originally wrote those same words while recording the case of David Davis but scratched out the word "filthy" and substituted "his own Lucer."[66]

Murderers had less verbiage devoted to their sins. When someone appeared before the circuit court for the taking of a life, the clerks expressed the horror of the state with rote phrases like "not having the fear of God before them" or "moved and seduced by the instigation of the Devil." Even other riots appeared in the record as "making such noise" for hours. The depth of the negative descriptions, their gendered use and the repetition in cases dealing specifically with "Bawdy houses" indicated how thoroughly the circuit court, and the city of Huntsville, despised them.

Mary Baker, Mary King and Ann Martin reappeared before the court in February 1821 for "passing and repassing in and along the public trails and common highways" of the city. They caused a disturbance on Sunday, May 7, when they gathered together "and tumultuously remained" for six hours. A small crowd "to the number of ten" formed around them. Although the circuit court attempted to prosecute them for disturbing the peace and never explicitly mentioned prostitution, this occurred five months after their dispersal from the "Bawdy house." That fact, and the court's language implying that their behavior damaged the moral fabric of the entire state, suggests that Baker, King and Martin were looking for customers. The jury fined them one dollar each.[67]

Rodah Barnett reappeared in the courtroom accused of opening and operating a second "Bawdy house" in April 1821. It attracted a diverse clientele, primarily people of "evil name fame and conversation" who congregated there "in the knight [*sic*] as in the day." Barnett diversified and operated her new "Bawdy house" as a brothel and local tavern or inn where her patrons spent their time "drinking, tippling, cursing swearing and otherwise misbehaving themselves." Throughout 1821, these women adapted to the new reality brought on by the closing of their former business and place of residence. In each instance, they survived however they could, as long as they could, until the circuit court stepped in to stop them. In April 1822, a jury found Barnett guilty of operating "a common ill governed and disorderly house" and fined her "one cent."[68]

This pattern plays out even with other "Bawdy houses" not operated by any of the original women. On April 1, 1821, the same day that Rodah Barnett was raided for the second time, the law took it upon itself to simultaneously shut down a "Bawdy house" run by Elizabeth King, who, like Barnett, appeared to regularly finance and operate taverns and brothels. In each instance, the circuit court described the perpetrators with specific hyperbolic phrases reserved for their profession and claimed that their existence threatened the morality and social order of the whole state. A jury then either dismissed the charges or gave the defendants symbolic fines. Although the aldermen and local reformers disliked the "public prostitutes," they found it difficult to convince juries that their presence was little more than a nuisance and a byproduct of city living.[69]

The prostitutes existed on the fringe of Huntsville's society, and like marginalized populations everywhere, people felt freer to attack them. Assaults on white women were uncommon in the circuit court records. This is not to say they did not occur. Domestic violence often appeared as a form of cruelty severe enough to initiate divorce proceedings, and there are a handful of assaults by white men on enslaved women. Yet these spinsters experienced far more non-spousal violence than any other group of women.

Jenning Seay attacked Mary King in June 1820. The court echoed itself in proclaiming that her life was "greatly despaired of," but this case differed from its predecessors in the steep fine demanded from Seay. The jurors assessed his fine to be "five hundred dollars," an amount that indicated brutal violence perpetrated on Mary King. Jeremiah Murphy and Lawrence Pendergrass attacked Elizabeth King, the aforementioned proprietor of a secondary "Bawdy house," on May 8, 1823.[70]

Court clerks often misspelled or misnamed women who appeared before them, using multiple names within the same case. Clerks wrote Rodah Barnett's name as "Rodah Barnard." They spelled Barbara Wilson's first name "Barbary" in an indictment. Even in a group of cases dealing directly with Mary Wilson, a court clerk referred to her as Mary Dillon for an entire page before correcting himself. Outside of this group of women, there are examples of court clerks using the feminine catchall "Polly" to refer to women in divorce cases. Women who appeared before the Madison County Circuit Court received little respect from its clerk. The court clerk occasionally spelled the surnames of men multiple ways in the same documents, occasionally listed aliases or used two names that sounded similar, but he never assigned them completely new ones. Thus, it is firmly in the realm of possibility that the unfortunate Mary Wilson, a habitual target of violence, was one of the Wilsons mentioned in the earliest indictments.

On September 8, 1820, a group of men and women attacked Mary Wilson. Robert Smith, Henry Ray (in later court cases, his name appeared as Rhea) and Mary Pratt all fell upon Wilson and "did beat wound and ill treat her." The court eventually dropped charges against Ray/Rhea but doggedly pursued both Smith and Pratt through multiple court terms. The court eventually dropped charges against them but not before attempting to recover a $250 bond placed on them to ensure their appearance at the next term of the court. Either Mary Pratt fled the county, or the clerk court changed her name to Fanny Cark or Mary Guttrie, both of whom later slipped away from Madison County, leaving Robert Smith alone to pay back the costs of the bond.

A similar group formed three months later on December 13, 1820. This time John Smith and Sarah Walker bludgeoned Mary Wilson with a variety of implements, including their own feet and hands but most notably "a cow shin" that they found nearby. Smith received a twenty-dollar fine for his assault on Wilson, and the repeated attacks may have been enough to dissuade her from remaining near Huntsville, because she, like the other women mentioned, soon faded away from the historic record.[71]

Prostitutes continued to operate in the city. Huntsville remained the largest settlement and one of the leading population centers of Alabama for the next two decades. The conditions that attracted women to the "Bawdy houses" in the 1820s existed until their eventual closings in the 1870s. Divorce cases from the period make mention of wives becoming an "inmate of a brothel" and of husbands bringing home venereal souvenirs from dalliances with a "certain class of fallen woman." However, the city no longer tried to prosecute prostitutes, nor did the state bring any further charges against them. All told, the prostitutes of early Huntsville survived. They survived the reformers of the early statehood period. They survived the assaults of strangers, clients and other single women. They persevered through tumultuous years and returned to relative anonymity after 1822. Although it was a dangerous life, they probably welcomed the opportunity to avoid the ire of the law and once against exist on the margins of a society that preferred to pretend they were not there.[72]

KIDNAPPING ON THE COTTON FRONTIER

Charles T. Collins ransacked homesteads, took hostages and stole livestock with equal abandon. He provoked the ire of his neighbors, and the brazen way in which he ignored the social contract shocked the court into taking severe penalties. His rampage began at the home of Nicholas Sheffield, a local coachmaker. Collins found a good horse, described by the court as "one bay gelding with foxed ears," worth about $100. He stole it. Now mounted and mobile, Collins surveyed Sheffield's home once more and came upon Tom. Tom was an enslaved person described as "one negro man…about thirty years of age" who belonged to Sheffield.

Now armed, on a horse and holding a hostage, Collins planned to sell. He pushed his rapidly fading luck. He traveled to the home of the brothers Thomas and William Brandon and kidnapped more enslaved people: "Edmund about twenty years of age and one Mulatto man named Lewis about twenty one years of age."

After this, Collins and his three-man coffle attempted to flee Madison County. They were quickly apprehended, and Collins appeared before the circuit court less than a month later to answer for a variety of charges, the most serious among them being "a True Bill of Indictment for slave stealing."[73]

The theft of human property carried heavy weight in early Alabama. Although court records referred to Collins and his attempt to "steal carry and take away" Tom, Edmund and Lewis with the same rote phrases used for the foxed-ear gelding or even an inanimate farm tool like a shovel, the enslaved men and their stolen labor were valued in the thousands, not tens or hundreds, of dollars. Their theft constituted a direct attack on the emerging middle and upper classes of the new cotton kingdom. As time passed, slave thefts continued, but as a crime that one did not inflict on their neighbors.

Instead of kidnapping enslaved people and transporting them from one end of the county to the other, bandits might go to Georgia or the Carolinas and march the hostages back.

However, the earliest days of Madison County witnessed the rampant kidnapping of both free and enslaved people alike. The first settlers possessed few communal feelings, and the county remained a lawless triangle until the mid-1810s. The earliest court records reveal a land where local slaveholders used kidnapping to ensure and expand their grotesque property rights.

On March 6, 1808, James Blair purchased three enslaved people—a man named Sam, a woman named Lucy and a "child named Mahala"—for $1,100. Nine months later, on Christmas Day 1808, Blair "casually lost" all three of them. One of his neighbors, William Wilborn, stumbled on the trio and claimed that "by finding" them he now owned them. Sam, Lucy and Mahala had escaped one slaveholder, only to be kidnapped by another. Blair claimed that Wilborn knew that the three belonged to him but that Wilborn "converted the aforesaid Negroes to his own use, and refused to deliver them."

Blair found himself unable to forcibly return Sam, Lucy and Mahala to his service, so he bided his time and sued Wilborn years later, introducing a suit in July 1811 that resulted in $330 in damages paid to Blair.

In 1810, James Burlison "trespass[ed] by taking away" two enslaved people—Stephen and Jane—from William Wilborn. The court could not find an unengaged prosecutor to try the case and released Burlison with a $500 bond if he failed to appear at the next term. Burlison fled with Stephen and Jane in tow. In January 1812, Wilborn instructed his lawyer, Marmaduke Williams, to present a note to the judge stating that because the county could not locate him, he no longer wished to prosecute Burlison for the theft.[74]

The July 1812 court session saw an additional pair of cases centered on kidnapping and slave theft. They involved two white men named Jesse Daniel and Claiborne Griffin, as well as four enslaved people: "Alotin Nancy Rachel and Abaline." In March 1811, Daniel attacked Griffin with clubs and staves. Once Daniel subdued him, he locked Griffin away for about a day.

Jesse Daniel alleged that he had assaulted the man because, days prior, Griffin had kidnapped Alotin, Nancy, Rachel and Abaline at sword point. Then he marched them to a place called "Bevers about four miles below Twickingham." There is the possibility that this refers to the Beaverdam area—an early cluster of cabins—but the geographic description is different from the Beaverdam found on later maps. Jurors reaffirmed their distaste toward slave theft by dismissing Griffin's kidnapping suit against Daniel and then charging Griffin eighty-seven dollars in fines for the brief amount of time he held Alotin, Nancy, Rachel and Abaline in "Bevers."[75]

The trend continued throughout the early 1810s. On June 16, 1812, William Blevins was "moved and seduced by the instigation of the devil" when he bought an enslaved woman named Beck from an unnamed trader who had stolen her from Louis Winston, an early prosecutor for the Mississippi Territory. Isaac Parrot did "steal and carry away" an unnamed enslaved man from Joseph Adams in August 1816. The men accused of slave theft often received punishment, the only exceptions being Isaac Parrot, whom the jurors found not guilty, and James Burlison, who fled rather than face the courts. Punishments ranged from hefty fines to simply declaring the guilty party return the kidnapped and pay court costs.[76]

However, few slave thefts occurred after Isaac Parrot's accused kidnapping of the unnamed man. The *Alabama Republican*, the main source of news for early Madison County, still reported on slave thefts, but these were kidnappings conducted by opportunists who targeted distant homesteads several miles from the city. No further slave thefts made it into the Madison County court records until Charles T. Collins went on his rampage in 1823.

The wording of his indictment also proved different. As previously mentioned, the circuit court used rote phrases in the body of Collins's cases. The court tried people for a variety of crimes, and when it issued indictments, it often used the fairly impartial phrase "A True Bill" or "True Bill of Indictment" followed by a brief description of the following legal battle. However, the court made an important distinction when it issued "A True Bill of Indictment for slave stealing." This terminology singled out Collins and his actions as being noteworthy to the law.

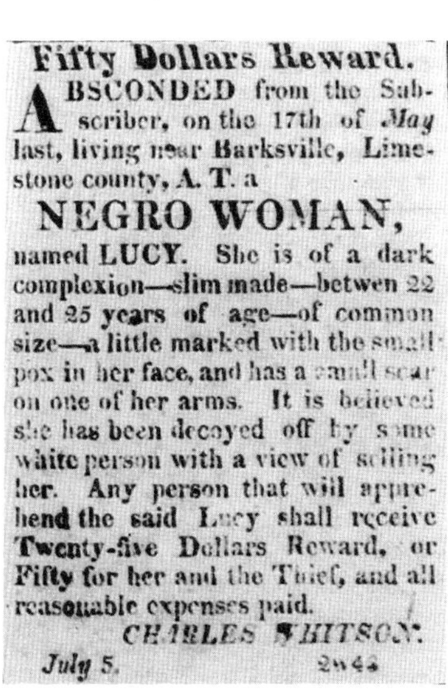

Fifty Dollars Reward.

ABSCONDED from the Subscriber, on the 17th of *May* last, living near Barksville, Limestone county, A. T. a

NEGRO WOMAN,

named LUCY. She is of a dark complexion—slim made—between 22 and 25 years of age—of common size—a little marked with the small-pox in her face, and has a small scar on one of her arms. It is believed she has been decoyed off by some white person with a view of selling her. Any person that will apprehend the said Lucy shall receive Twenty-five Dollars Reward, or Fifty for her and the Thief, and all reasonable expenses paid.

CHARLES WHITSON.

July 5. 2w44

The theft of Lucy. *Courtesy of the Madison County Special Collections.*

Collins faced three consecutive trials. In each, the court read a description of his crimes, and Collins pleaded not guilty several times. The judge asked him if any extenuating circumstances existed that should prevent the full fury of the law from coming down on him. Collins, possibly dreading the hefty fines to come, put on a brave face and declared "that he has nothing to say but that he has before said."

The jurors returned three separate times. For the theft of the foxed-ear gelding horse, Collins had to pay $300. He probably balked at the heft of the fine for stealing a simple horse, but the judge was not done with his sentencing. In addition to the fine, Collins would be taken from the courtroom and between 2:00 and 4:00 p.m. "receive on his bare back thirty nine stripes well laid on." After all of this, the court declared that Collins be branded on his right hand with the letter *T* to signify to all the world he was a thief. Once he had been beaten and branded, the sheriff would then drag him to the county jail, where he would reside for the next six months.

The next jury walked in. It found Collins guilty of the theft of Edmund and Lewis. The judge shortened his six-month sentence by declaring he leave the "close confinement" of the county jail on the "first Friday in December next." Rather than being released, the sheriff and a few constables would take Collins to "some convenient place" between 10:00 a.m. and 2:00 p.m. on December 1, 1820, and hang him.

5

DIVORCES

Introduction

Family served as the economic and social foundation of the nineteenth-century United States. American settlers arrived in caravans of families. Americans considered marriage a sacred and essential institution, as it was the only accepted way to create new families and fuse preexisting ones. Once entered into, a family proved incredibly difficult to leave.

In early America, most states required permission from a state legislature to divorce. Thus, the records of state legislatures from New York to Louisiana are often replete with private bills deciding the fates of an individual household. A variety of types of divorce existed; *mensa et thoro*, or "bed and board divorce," allowed the couple to live apart from each other and manage their own property but forbade them to ever remarry. Most divorces in antebellum Alabama were of this "bed and board" kind. A second form of divorce, *a vinculo matrimonii*, granted a total and complete legal separation. The two parties might not only live apart but also remarry and create a new family. Such a divorce proved rare and was granted only when one party provided proof of overwhelming injustice.

Despite the cost, the uncertainty of success and the social stigma associated with being a divorced person, the action of divorce proved increasingly popular in the young republic because it provided legal protection for property. Absent spouses racked up debts, and creditors called on their next of kin. To prevent money problems, abandoned wives and husbands

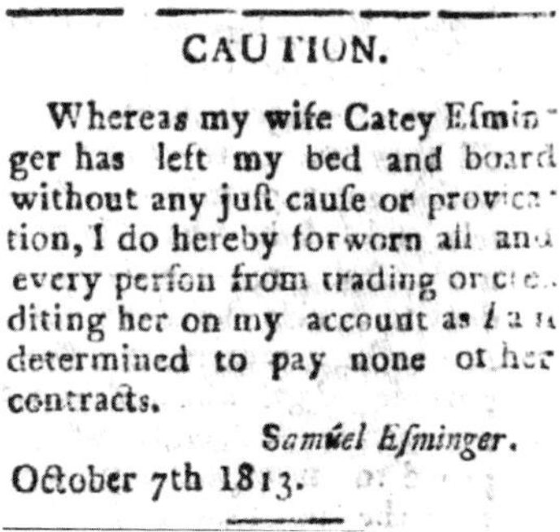

CAUTION.

Whereas my wife Catey Eſminger has left my bed and board without any juſt cauſe or provocation, I do hereby forworn all and every perſon from trading or crediting her on my account as I am determined to pay none of her contracts.

Samuel Eſminger.

October 7th 1813.

NOTICE.

I FOREWARN all persons trading with my wife D lila Standefer, on any account, as I will not pay any debts of her contracting, she left my bed and board without out any provocation.

WM. STANDEFER.

Nov. 20. 1t*

Left: Esminger contract notice. *Right*: William Standefer notice. *Courtesy of the Madison County Special Collections.*

advertised in local newspapers that they would no longer honor contracts the errant spouse made.

A dual system developed along the Atlantic Seaboard whereby spouses petitioned both the courts and the legislatures within the same state, resulting in a patchwork of divorce laws that occasionally conflicted with themselves. To remedy the mess, most states eventually scrapped any legislative requirements and allowed local courts to oversee matters. By the beginning of the American Civil War, only Alabama still required legislative approval for divorce.

Most power devolved to the courts, and by the 1850s, the legislature often existed as a rubber stamp for local judges. Yet the practice remained that legislators in Montgomery voted on each divorce and possessed the opportunity to intercede in the affairs of the household if they wished. It was not until the secession constitution in 1861 that Alabama relegated divorce to the courts.

Divorces often included property lists, witness testimonies and compelling narratives—intimate insights into the lives of all social classes in white nineteenth-century North Alabama. Although Madison County had a small free Black population, there are no divorce cases involving the county's free people of color. The Black residents mentioned in North Alabama divorce cases are all enslaved and appear as property fought over as fiercely as land and cattle. They do, however, occasionally appear as mistresses, handmaidens and confidants to the white population.

Ultimately, divorce cases provided a look into the workings of individual families in a specific place and time. The evidence assembled by spouses against one another rivals wills and census records in providing an understanding of the economic life of families, while the (sometimes literal) blow-by-blow accounts of feuds provide an insight into the lives of the middle classes and the poor—groups that rarely left behind the diaries that many historians have used to reconstruct daily life. Finally, the cases had to present a compelling narrative, one that would move the heart not only of the local judge but also of a group of men in Tuscaloosa or Montgomery who had never met any of the participants listed. Such stories still speak to us across the ages.[77]

ROUNTREE VERSUS ROUNTREE

In the early 1790s, William and Sally Rountree met and married in the "District of Lawrence" of South Carolina. Those familiar with South Carolina's geography will note that there is no Lawrence County. It seems likely that the court clerk or one of the attached attorneys heard Sally Rountree say "Laurens"—one of the new counties created in 1785—and simply wrote down "Lawrence."

After residing in western South Carolina for close to ten years, the couple headed for the newly purchased lands along the southern rim of the cotton frontier. Their claims about their arrival in Madison County, like so many other things, are similar but contradictory. Sally claims that William Rountree arrived in Madison County in 1809, "carrying with him your oratrix and his family." William Rountree himself placed the event at a far hazier "eleven or twelve years [ago]."

William Rountree distinguished himself from his arrival in the county. In a land full of squatters and small holds, the Rountrees emerged as early members of the frontier elite. In the 1811 Tax List, he owned 310 acres of good land near the Flint River, in the eastern part of the county, and no slaves. For all this land he paid but fifty-five cents in tax. William next appears in 1813, with 320 acres and eight newly acquired enslaved people, all situated along the Flint. The conflicting Rountree suits reveal a glimpse of the daily lives of the more prosperous inhabitants of the county. Through their arguments we can learn what was expected of parents, spouses and extended family when wealthy men faltered in public view.[78]

In 1822, William Rountree brought a divorce suit against Sally Rountree claiming that, in 1816, he traveled to North Carolina "to purchase some negroes for some elder children" who had recently married. It is likely that William intended these enslaved persons for a daughter, either as dowry or property in her own right. White women from wealthier families engaged in and benefited directly from the slave trade; prenuptial and postnuptial agreements regarding human property were common among the wealthy in the antebellum South. Sons often got their inheritance in cash or land, while daughters received people.[79]

So, for his (likely) daughter's marriage, William Rountree traveled to North Carolina for about three months. As he made the trek back, enslaved persons in tow, he stopped to rest at an inn on Cumberland Mountain. It was most likely the Stand at Fall Creek, the first inn operated by local businesswoman Mary Haley. There he ran into Sally Rountree and "her little son," on their way to the Carolinas. He spoke to her briefly and learned "to his astonishment that she intended to leave him." According to William's original testimony, for no discernible reason, she took one of their youngest children and embarked from their home near Huntsville, intercepted him near Crossville, Tennessee, and continued on from there to her father's home in the Upstate region of South Carolina.

Sally, of course, had a different recollection of events.

She claimed that in 1814, two years prior to their meeting on the mountain, she had indeed traveled to South Carolina after learning of her mother's death to visit family and offer help to her grieving father. After spending two months with family in South Carolina, Sally Rountree returned to the Mississippi Territory, where she claims to have found William "suffering under a complaint commonly called the pock or clap." According to Sally, William contracted the illness from his "illicit commerce with women of ill fame and prostitute characters." The pock, "being of a contagious nature," was then easily "communicated to [her] on her first reception" on returning home. She described the affliction as being "tormented." William called on one Dr. Higginbotham to inspect and diagnose her ills. Sally made ready mention in her divorce suit that, due to her husband's alleged negligence, she was "indecently exposed to effect a cure."

After recovering from the infection, she vowed to no longer live with him and returned to South Carolina for three or four years. Thus, in Sally's retelling of the end of their marriage, they never met on a mountain.

William readily admitted that she suffered from an ailment but asserted that she contracted it after she left home to visit her family in 1812, contradicting her 1814 travel claims, and he found her already afflicted on her return from South Carolina. In fact, William claimed he overheard Dr. Higginbotham, during his previously mentioned examination, say that Sally "ought to be bled and take a dose of salts"

Crab Apple Inn. *Courtesy of the Cumberland County Archives.*

to cure what ailed her. Sally protested loudly, claiming, "if it were not the foul disorders" she should recover without the use of medicine fairly shortly. She recuperated and resided with William until 1816, when he "went eastwards" to North Carolina.

Though they often vehemently denied the recollections of the other party, both agreed that William "wrote several letters" pleading with Sally to return home, one of which eventually persuaded her to make the trip back to Madison County. Again, their recounting of the letters differs. Sally claimed she felt for William as he attempted to raise the "infant child of his son." Caring for their grandchild alone, the offspring of one of their sons and a woman "who had no place of residence" was difficult on the aging William. Sally agreed to leave South Carolina to assist with this burden so long as she could take a separate room. In return for her help, William vowed to "quit his illicit amor with a certain class of abandoned women." William claimed that she eventually returned to Alabama because he "sent her $50."

In fact, William Rountree never spoke of the aforementioned "infant child of his son" and said that although she returned to Madison County, she spent several years with her "daughters in Limestone [County]." It appears from the records—like an 1822 writ of subpoena sent to the sheriff of Lauderdale County commanding him to summon Sally Rountree for her initial court appearance—that she lived among her married children and their spouses, spending time at each household before moving to the next. In this manner, she managed to avoid William for years until no more married children remained and she at last returned home. William put her up in a separate room and tried to woo her often, but she ignored him and refused "all intercourse of a conjugal character."

Neither one of them found joy in this situation, and Sally began to mention her desire to move again. So, exhausted and out of options to provide for his wife, William Rountree sued for divorce in July 1822. It proved a short case, and William dismissed his own bill in February 1823, as he believed he had reached an agreeable alimony settlement with Sally Rountree and established Zedekiah Pate, one of his sons-in-law, as the trustee in charge of it.

Although William thought the whole issue settled, Sally had other plans. She initiated her own divorce suit against William a month later on April 29, 1823. She asserted that William promised half of his estate to her "provided she would hold her peace and not expose him" regarding his alleged dalliances with prostitutes. She accepted this large sum as "compensation for [her] silence."

Now, William had delivered some property prior to this second divorce suit. He gave her an enslaved young woman, a $500 bond and a bed, all of which William delivered to her son-in-law's home in either Limestone or Lauderdale County. She demanded more and viewed a human life, furniture and several years' salary for the average laborer as insufficient maintenance, claiming it was "a very small part of his large fortune scarcely amounting to one twentieth."

William was furious and responded that he had given her far more alimony than she claimed. According to his rebuttal, he had tried to match the wealth she had as a single woman in South Carolina, saying that Sally "ought to have as much property" as she brought into the marriage. In addition to the enslaved woman and the bed, he also furnished her a "valuable saddle horse worth $180" and a whole variety of bedsteads and chests. He had already paid part of the $500 bond for her use and subsequently viewed the whole case as a farce, ranting that "the conduct of a perverse woman baffles all calculation" and that all the drama arose from the "phantoms of her own disordered imagination."

The court agreed. William had produced the contract between himself and Zedekiah Pate dated November 18, 1822, which outlined all the payments made and the property transferred from one man to the other. It was this negotiation between her husband and her son-in-law that sealed Sally Rountree's fate.

Sally knew about the contract because she took part in the negotiations. Early on in the process, William had only offered her $300 to sustain her the rest of her life. Pate, the son-in-law, pressured her to take it. He argued that it was a fair amount. Sally refused. She spent years circulating among her married children and understood that few things were permanent or safe when others owned your property. As a buffer, she demanded $500, which, if her son-in-law proved a little reckless, would still get her further than the $300.

As records of their marriage differ so wildly, it is impossible to say whose recollection proved closer to the truth. However, the Rountree cases stand out in a variety of ways. Sally proved able to travel widely and reside with family when her marriage fell apart, an option unavailable to most white women in early Alabama. Neither of the Rountrees called on witnesses for their case, although witnesses often formed the backbone of divorce suits initiated by less prosperous citizens. Both Rountrees relied on their own good word as long-settled and wealthy residents of the county to carry weight in the courts. Sally put her energy into trying to publicly attack William's reputation. William denied her allegations and relied on the contract he filed with the clerk's office to carry him through. In the end, the Rountree divorces provide a window into the strategies the wealthier citizens of North Alabama used to win court cases. While poor whites produced shocking scandals and eyewitness testimony, the wealthy relied on their reputation and careful documentation to carry the day.

It must have not come as much of a surprise to Sally Rountree when the judge dismissed her petition for divorce. She knew about the contract and knew that contracts signed by rich men carried weight. She probably expected the judge to stop after he ruled the contract valid. But, in an extraordinary step, he declared William's original divorce petition valid and proclaimed the "bonds of Matrimony" existing between them "be now and henceforth forever dissolved."[80]

William Rountree won his cause in her case.

HALL VERSUS HALL

Nathaniel Hall married Mary Wiley in 1812. By contemporary standards, they had a good marriage—in their twenty-six years together, they amassed more than one hundred acres of land, had ten children and owned enough livestock to put up "10 or 12 hundred pounds of bacon" for the winter.

According to their divorce cases, it had been going poorly since 1818. The civil suits of Nathaniel Hall and Mary Hall offer a vivid insight into the domestic and economic lives of a yeoman family. Although they owned their own land, possessed plenty of hogs and cattle and had three slaves, their contemporaries still described them as a family "of modest circumstances" who occasionally needed to barter and borrow to purchase essentials like salt, clothing and coffee.

The Hall family fell somewhere between the migratory white laborers who drifted across the South and the middle-class merchants and factory owners who employed them and extended them credit. Though they owned slaves, they were far from the plantation aristocracy of Virginia, the Carolinas and the Black Belt. Their children attended school, though it appears that both parents were illiterate. They planned for a brighter future for the generations who came after them but worked their own land in the present. The Halls were members of the largest class of property owners in the antebellum South—what historians call the "plain folk."

Mary and Nathaniel Hall pursued separate divorce cases against each other, produced multiple character witnesses who possessed detailed recollections of events and performed cross-examinations when their own lawyers were not present.

Their children, neighbors and business partners split off into opposing camps, which generally favored or disparaged one of the parties involved. However, even partisan witnesses highlighted a social good. This allowed a fuller picture of the Halls to emerge. Although Mary Hall may have had other lovers, she was often careful with the family finances. Though Nathaniel sometimes yelled at his wife, every witness described him as a loving father who provided well for the family. The following examination is a synthesis of these two extremes, one that hopefully captures the truth that lies between.

In 1818, moved by an internal compass, Mary Hall briefly fled her home and responsibilities in Madison County. According to both her husband's deposition and the testimony of William Dotery and John Bales, she "eloped with one Martin Guest," a neighbor, and "fled to parts unknown." When questioned as to who exactly claimed she fled her home, both Dotery and Bales responded that it was "a common neighborhood talk." Rumors about her chastity and conduct circulated widely throughout their section of Madison County, fueled by her long absence with Guest. On her return, Nathaniel seemed ready to end the whole marriage there and then but found mercy and accepted the reality of her temporary desertion through "the interposition of friends and on her promises of Reformation."

Although she returned to her life in Madison County, her behavior still fueled speculation and "neighborhood talk" about her chastity. Joseph Short testified to "seeing her with my own eyes get in bed with" James McCartney. Short watched for several hours as they acted "as man and wife the bigger part of the night."

Faced with all this unyielding scrutiny, Mary Hall became increasingly blunt about her dalliances. During a later conversation with the same Joseph Short, he began "joking her" that she had grown too old to keep up her affairs and other "old tricks." She denied his accusations about her lack of vigor and told him "there were two or three young men come to see her… younger than her own son."

Zebulon Glasscock also witnessed this behavior. Sometime "about two to five years back," he watched a local doctor named John Morgan visit the Hall residence and "act as man and wife" with Mary. In fact, he may have participated in an affair with her himself. During his own testimony, he mentioned "other evidences that I could give but I cannot with criminating myself."

Glasscock mentioned a second man, William Boyd, as having committed adulterous relations with Mary Hall around the same time as Dr. Morgan. Boyd denied having ever spent the night at the Hall residence alongside both Morgan and Mary Hall, but other witnesses reported him visiting her at the homes of neighbors to "have some private conversation" while trying to "evade" the homeowners. Ultimately, in Nathaniel Hall's countersuit, he named Boyd and Morgan by name and accused them both of carrying on relations with Mary that lasted until the present day.

In the spring of 1838, John Heathcock found Mary Hall wandering the roads of their neighborhood "about dark something like four miles from her home." She asked him to help her search for a piece of lost property. He agreed to assist her, but when they arrived back at the Hall residence, he saw a stranger on horseback. He told the court, "As I approached him he moved further from me in order that I should not speak to or recognize him."

After many years of brazen adultery on her part, the rumors and "neighborhood talk" that swirled around Mary Hall finally reached her husband. According to Nathaniel's account, he "remonstrated with her." Though based on later depositions in which witnesses described "rough language" between them, his remonstration probably proved more contentious than a simple chiding.

Mary Hall responded by stabbing him.

Apparently, she stabbed him more than once. Samuel J. House testified that he had "known her to stab the defendant on two separate occasions"

French Dagger Under Pillow. Illustration by Sha-Meika Smith.

and casually mentioned that he "discovered a large French Dirk calculated to produce death" concealed under the head of Mary's bed.

When James Ragsdale visited the Halls, he spoke with Mary in a hallway. When Nathaniel "came out of the room into the passage and gave her abusive language," he then left the home and continued his conversation with Nathaniel outside. Nathaniel asked Ragsdale if he had seen him drop his pistol. Ragsdale replied that he had not. Nathaniel responded by "unbuttoning his pantaloons" to show him the pistol he hid on himself at all times as well as a knife wound "given a long time ago by the appearance of the scar," left behind by Mary Hall.

Ragsdale asked him why he kept a pistol at all times. Nathaniel explained that his sons routinely "presented guns against him" and had on occasion threatened his life.

In early May 1838, Nathaniel finally caught Mary "alone with a man in the woods." According to his deposition, they reclined in a compromised position, one that convinced him that they had recently finished their "illicit interview." He left the home, resolved never again to reside with Mary and moved in with his brother about a mile away.

A little over a month later, Nathaniel Hall returned "to superintend some of his plantation affairs." He traveled with a friend; Nathaniel made sure that all of his later run-ins with his wife and sons took place in front of witnesses. Although Nathaniel fails to mention the specific friend in question, based on the collection of testimonies, it is most likely that Logan D. Brandon traveled with him.

Brandon not only accompanied Nathaniel Hall to his home in June 1838, he also emerged as a frequent business partner. Based on Brandon's appearances in the court records, he seems to be a man who derived much of his income from hiring out the enslaved. In Mary Hall's opening petition, she specifically names Brandon as in the process of buying the Hall family's three enslaved people. Unfortunately, the Halls failed to ever mention their names and list only their ages; a man about the age of sixty, a fifteen-year-old girl and a thirteen-year-old boy. Nathaniel attempted to sell all three to Logan Brandon for $1,460. Later in the year, when it was time to crib the corn and clear the fields, Nathaniel hired an enslaved man named Sam from Brandon to replace his labor on the farm.

The reconstruction of this event from textual evidence is complicated. Both Mary and Nathaniel accused the other of presenting guns and threatening murder, and both of the Halls produced a witness who corroborated their version of events. Andrew Hall claimed that his father pulled a pistol on his mother and "swore by all that was good and bad that if she did not give up the negroes he would blow her brains out." Brandon later testified that he saw Andrew Hall "present a gun at [Nathaniel]…said to be heavily charged with buck shot."

Later encounters between Nathaniel Hall and his sons lend credence to his and Brandon's assertion that nineteen-year-old Andrew Hall, a young man "alledged to be of weak intellect," might have threatened to shoot his father. In the spring of 1838, one of Nathaniel's younger sons, thirteen-year-old Alexander Hall, escorted him onto the farm. William F. Hall met them near the cornfields.

William F. Hall is an interesting part of the case. He sued on behalf of Mary Hall as her next friend and later testified against Nathaniel Hall: "I have heard him in time threaten [Mary]…and I have seed him strike her." Yet he is not listed by the neighbor Valentine Hill as being one of the boys left behind to bring in the crops alone after Nathaniel moved to his brother's home. Based on William's closeness to the case and knowledge of the Halls' domestic affairs it is most likely he is an older son, over the age of twenty-one, who kept a house elsewhere in the county—an older son with a long-burning grudge against his father.

So, when Mary and William found Nathaniel and Alexander in the corn, it proved a tense situation, one that ended with William pulling a cocked gun on his father as he "swore that he would kill the first man that took an ear of corn from there." On a second occasion, Nathaniel returned to his family's home in the presence of Robert Bailey. Nathaniel came to ask for the keys to his home, and according to Bailey, William Hall "threatened to kill or whip [Nathaniel] or have him killed if he did not keep away from there." To add insult to threatened injury, Mary Hall used this opportunity to inform Nathaniel that "her children were bastards."

Additionally, when Nathaniel Hall returned on a fourth occasion to collect items, this time accompanied by Steven Provence, John Hall, his seventeen-year-old son, found him by the corncrib and said "bitterly" that "if [the] defendant came any nearer he would kill him."

The evidence points to Nathaniel Hall and Logan D. Brandon's recollection being more accurate. However, several witnesses, notably the aforementioned William F. Hall, noted that in later years Nathaniel struck Mary in front of them and "very rough conversation" often took place between them.

Disturbed by Nathaniel's repeated attempts to return home and financed in her suit by her older son, William F. Hall, Mary petitioned for a divorce *a mensa et thoro* on June 25, 1838. She accused Nathaniel of possessing "unfounded resentment" and of conspiring to slowly starve the family into submission by not providing more financial support. She also claimed that Nathaniel recently returned home and managed to steal all of her weapons before she caught him leaving the house. On his discovery, he allegedly told her "that he was well armed with *pistols* & that he intendid her time in this world should be very short."

Mary Hall appealed to the court's sense of paternal obligation. She pointed out that she still cared for many young children on her own, including Andrew Hall, one of the sons witnessed pulling guns on Nathaniel. She claimed that Andrew was "of intellect so weak that he is incapable of taking care of himself." How could she juggle all this responsibility, she pleaded, without alimony with which to support herself and the remaining children?

Nathaniel penned a quick response. Rather than focus on the threats of violence to himself and others, his first refutation was that Andrew possessed enough cognitive skills to avoid being an additional burden. "It is true," he conceded, "that he is not as sprightly as some of the other children, but he is fully able to take care of himself and capable of doing as valuable service on the plantation as any other young man."

Later in his response, after listing the manifold violence done to him, he zeroed in on the crux of the issue. How could he offer additional support to Mary and the children when they already possessed the whole of his plantation, "on which there is a comfortable dwelling house, all necessary out houses and more than one hundred acres cleared"? He did not object to providing all the necessary things for his family but insisted that all they needed lay in front of them. He asserted that it was not the resources that might be found lacking but the capacity of the one left in charge of their administration.

After all the violence and deceit and infidelity, the thing that upset him the most was Mary's perceived frivolity. Indeed, if length of complaint and number of questions posed to witnesses correlates with the importance of the issue, then Nathaniel Hall was far more concerned about reports that Mary "sold a large quantity of bacon…and that she is permitting his stock of hogs and cattle to be wasted" than he ever was about being stabbed by his wife or nearly murdered by his own sons.

As for the conspiracy to slowly starve the family into submission, two neutral witnesses mentioned offhand utterances by Nathaniel that might support this assertion. James Ragsdale, during the same visit in which Nathaniel unbuttoned his pants to show him a scar, heard Nathaniel mention that because his sons had pulled guns on him in the past he would like to sell his property to force the younger ones "to go to him for support," and he wanted to buy a second property away from Mary Hall and his elder sons "and put his small children upon it." Additionally, during a conversation with Benjamin A. Rickets, Nathaniel mentioned how he found his family ungrateful and that "if they got anything their hands should know how they got it."

Ultimately, neither Mary nor Nathaniel wished to live together any longer. They had spent twenty-six years together, most of them contentious, and no-fault divorce had yet to become the norm in the United States. In Mary's bill, she sought a divorce of bed and board, an arrangement that would provide her with alimony but prevent either of them from ever remarrying. Nathaniel simply sought for Mary's bill to be dismissed. It eventually was around Christmas 1839.

As soon as Nathaniel proved financially able, he retaliated with a divorce suit of his own. In May 1841, he alleged that while the previous suit worked its way through the chancery court, Mary (whose name appeared in the second divorce petition as Polly) "had adulterous intercourse" again with both William Boyd and John Morgan.

Subpoenas were issued and sheriffs were informed to summon witnesses. All the gears of the court started turning for a second round, but tragically, on June 16, 1841, Nathaniel Hall came to court to inform them that Mary Hall had died.[81]

Hall versus Hall offered no catharsis. There would never be a brief moment of exhalation as a judge either freed one side or doomed both by continuing their marital bonds to each other. A case as convoluted and fascinating as this—it attracted every gossip in the neighborhood, contained impassioned defenses over the price of bacon and pitted sons against (probable) father—could not possibly end without a twist.

Until the end, Nathaniel seemed to love both Mary and his family, describing their time together prior to her infidelities and his sons' hatred of him as an "uninterrupted harmony." No, Mary's death probably provided little relief to Nathaniel, but it probably put an end to all that "neighborhood talk."

Layman versus Layman

Rebecca Byram stood at an altar in Shelby County in February 1818. She gazed at John Layman and considered her new life with uncertainty and guessed at what lay before her. On this day, she planned to marry John, a man she never loved.

Shortly after their marriage, they headed north, to the hustle and bustle of Madison County, where John hoped to live in "domestic comfort & felicity" with his new bride. However, Rebecca failed to relish married life in the way John hoped she might. John Layman continued to try. He showered her with praise in an effort to "conciliate her esteem." He doted as best he could in the hopes that she might soon come around and they could both "cherish that reciprocity of affection so essential to…a conubial life." All of his attempts failed to persuade her, and his dream of a happy marriage was "soon blasted."

Then came the day when he grew "suddenly & violently ill." Apparently moved by the plight of her husband, Rebecca became "uncommonly tender" in her care. She cooked for him, helped him to bed and brought him rum. Rebecca instructed John "in an affectionate manner & tone" to drink deeply in the hopes that the liquor might break the fever or at least numb his discomfort. Moved by her sudden reversal in manners, John drank the draught. He quickly discovered that "instead of rum" she had brought him an entire cup of "elixir of vitriol."

Elixir of vitriol was a popular tincture used to treat a wide variety of conditions in the eighteenth and nineteenth centuries. According to

William Buchan's *Domestic Medicine*, one of the first home remedy books in the English-speaking world, elixir of vitriol treated myriad conditions like intestinal worms, loss of appetite and flatulence. Made from mixing oil of vitriol with spirits and often served in quantities of thirty drops for a whole cup of water or wine, elixir of vitriol was so powerful that remedy books suggested serving it in a glass tube and rinsing the mouth after ingestion so that the medicine could not damage the teeth. The physicians who wrote these books treated the tincture so carefully because its main ingredient, oil of vitriol, was an archaic name for sulfuric acid.[82]

When John Layman finally tasted the elixir of vitriol, he immediately knew it was not rum. Luckily, the "potency of the liquor had…been exhausted" or the dosage of elixir of vitriol he drank would have killed him. When John told Rebecca, she became "much confused" and claimed it had been an accident. It was a claim he believed until her departure a few months later.

She grew increasingly "irritable & abusive" until, one night in October 1818, Rebecca finally told John the truth. She never loved him. When they first wed, she did not love him. When they moved across the state, she did not love him. At no point during their time together had she felt any real matrimonial affection; ultimately, "she had no regard for him." She married John under the "expectation that she could afterwards love him," but that expectation proved too great. Rebecca confessed that she was "discontented" and planned to leave as soon as she could. John pleaded with her to stay, but a month later, she took all the "effects she had brought in marriage" and set out. He pleaded with her to return but eventually found "all efforts to reclaim her ineffectual."[83]

Rebecca Layman taking the property she brought into the marriage might seem barely worth mentioning, but the action directly contradicted the legal underpinnings of marriage at the time. Prior to 1839, no state had passed statutes allowing married women to own or manage their own property. The United States inherited the concept of coverture from British common law—it was the doctrine that, on marriage, a woman transformed from a *feme sole* or single woman entirely capable of owning property and running a business into a *feme covert*, or covered woman, whose entire legal existence was now inseparable from that of her husband. In exchange for paltry legal protections, a feme covert could not be sued; she gave up the right to property. Nuptial agreements occasionally protected the property a woman brought into the marriage, but these rarely existed among poor whites, and a husband might live elsewhere and occasionally return to confiscate the property a wife had accrued by wage labor between absences. A contemporary example is

Elizabeth Smith, whose husband, Ezekiel, abandoned the family and returned to Kentucky, only to return every six months and "appropriate to intemperance the small sums which she had earned."

Other divorces from North Alabama mentioned a wife taking money, clothes or furniture as payment from her husband during a separation, but no other case specifically mentioned a woman retrieving what she brought into the marriage and leaving with it. She might have attempted to poison her husband; domestic violence was not rare among people seeking divorces in the nineteenth century. However, her decision to openly admit her lack of feelings for her husband, a rare enough event, coupled with her reclamation of property, proved radical concepts on the early nineteenth-century southern frontier. The court took pity on John Layman and, in 1827, granted him a full divorce.

COLEMAN VERSUS COLEMAN

In August 1836, a "Theatrical Company" arrived in Huntsville. It planned to perform "An Entertainment" for the locals consisting of "Recitations, Imitations, Songs etc. etc. etc." at the theater on the corner of Lincoln and Clinton Streets. Among the performers was an actor named Henry Riley, described in his olio as a former manager at "many of the principal theatres in the Union."

Riley listed a variety of performances in his show. He planned to perform his own renditions of celebrated scenes from the works of Shakespeare, Sheridan, Home and Southrey. Riley followed these with his best imitations of more famous English and American actors, including a performance as the famous Welsh actress Sarah Siddons as Lady Randolph in the play *Douglas*. He ended the evening with a series of comic songs and humorous stories like "Butter and Cheese," "Yorkshireman's Visit to London" and "Tippitty Witchet."

Tickets were fifty cents, children paid half price and Riley made sure the "Front seats [were] reserved for the Ladies." During a performance, one of the ladies in the front row caught Henry Riley's eye.

Emiline Coleman was young—either twenty-one or twenty-two at the time of their meeting—and quite impressed by the talented actor from out of town. She lived next door—her garden and privy bordered the back half of the theater lot—and she might have been a frequent visitor there. Henry Riley introduced himself, and they began passing notes to each other,

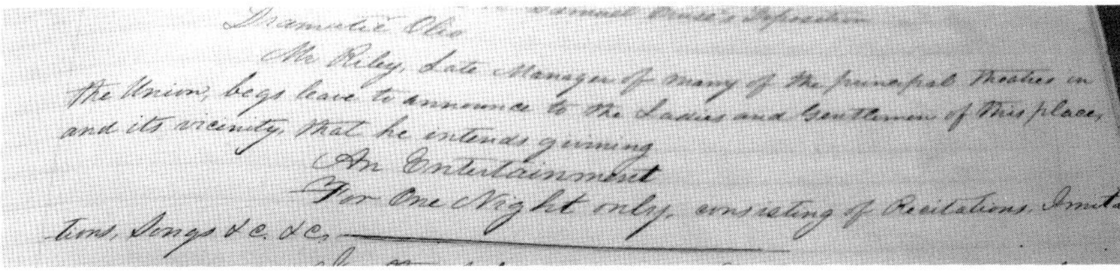

Dramatic Olio
Mr Riley, late Manager of many of the principal Theatres in the Union, begs leave to announce to the Ladies and Gentlemen of this place, and its vicinity, that he intends giving
An Entertainment
For One Night only, consisting of Recitations, Imitations, Songs &c. &c.

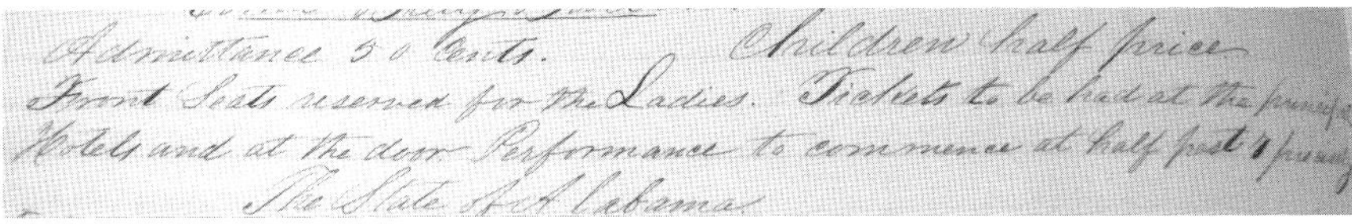

Admittance 50 Cents. Children half price
Front Seats reserved for the Ladies. Tickets to be had at the principal Hotels and at the door. Performance to commence at half past 7 precisely
The State of Alabama

Top: Dramatic Olio A. *Bottom*: Dramatic Olio B. *Courtesy of the Madison County Probate Archives.*

leaving them in fence posts, dropping them from windows or stashing little declarations of love in other secret locations around town. Emiline even used enslaved women as couriers.

Only Emiline's letters to Henry Riley survived to enter the chancery court records. As young and refreshing as their fling might have been, it was still an affair.

Emiline had married John Coleman seven years earlier on Christmas Eve 1829. They wed in Courtland, a small town in Lawrence County, which once served as an important stop on the stagecoach routes that ran from Nashville to Mobile. Emiline had traveled a long way to her new home. Depositions from the Coleman household and court documents list her as being from Marengo County, a land of vast cotton plantations, Bonapartist refugees and recently abandoned vineyards. However, Emiline's records indicate that she was from Greensboro, a town in Greene County, north of the French Grant.

When they wed in December 1829, Emiline was a scant fifteen years old and far from home. John was twenty-five. She had few friends in this new land; his sisters served as her bridesmaids. They all soon removed to the family home about a mile or so outside of Huntsville, and Emiline spent the first years of married life in a house with her new husband, his two older sisters and their mother—at least until Mother Coleman's death in 1831.

In 1834, Emiline and John moved into Huntsville, to a house on the corner of Randolph and Green Streets. He began practicing law and set to "making money rapidly." The next year, John's two sisters, Narcissa and Delia, followed them into the city, buying their own home not far from the couple. The sisters visited often, and much of Emiline's social life consisted of John's extended family, a handful of other married women and the household's enslaved women. Emiline spent much of her time with a young woman named Ann, whom she described as "her favorite girl."

Narcissa disliked Emiline. She revealed in later testimony that she found John Coleman "foolishly fond" of his young bride, and she publicly expressed her fears that he would "ruinously embarrass himself" in purchasing Emiline all the luxuries of a wealthy lawyer's wife. She reported that in 1836 alone he spent a considerable sum on a "Piano Forte," a variety of jewelry and a "great number of valuable and expensive articles of Dress."

So, with the bulk of her social interactions dominated by a much older husband whose immediate family members openly expressed their disdain for her, there is little surprise that Emiline found the well-traveled actor next door so irresistible.

According to the recollections of witnesses, their affair began around the first of September, after Henry Riley and his "theatrical company" had already been in the city for two weeks. The court is unclear of the date of their first meeting, so there may have been a prolonged period of seduction before they began passing notes, or they may have had an immediate chemistry.

Either way, early in their infatuation, Emiline penned brief letters to Riley like the following:

> *Come after tea here and I will come down to the garden.*
> *Henry If you will come down to the theatre this evening I will go there and tell you where you may see me. Let no one of this, not for your life. Mr. C is in the country. I am alone.*

An affair this intense could not help but attract attention, and it appears the enslaved people of Huntsville were the first to notice a rich man's wife stealing kisses from a stranger. One of the closest enslaved people to the center of the melodrama was Ann.

Ann is an interesting participant in the divorce, and the only sketch of her comes from a line in Narcissa's testimony in which she describes the young woman as "13 or 14 years of age, worth at that time 800$ at least." Emiline stated in her earliest letters to Henry Riley that Ann would direct him where to wait for her, and the enslaved girl occasionally acted as a chaperone when Emiline took a stagecoach south to visit family. Ann filled a role akin to a handmaiden. Thus, Ann knew the details of much of Emiline's life. From the latter's letters to Henry, we know that Ann occasionally appeared in Emiline's dreams. Although Ann spent much of her time as Emiline's handmaiden, Narcissa spoke of the fact that Emiline "has her yet," which implied that Ann was originally attached to the Coleman household, and that, in addition to all she did for Emiline, she may have had one more job: domestic spy for John's sisters. It is possible that on September 9, 1836, when Narcissa and Delia learned of "reports…whispered about amongst the negroes" questioning Emiline's chastity and exposing details of her weeklong affair with Henry, the "reports" may have emanated from Ann.

When Delia heard the rumors circulating among the enslaved and learned of the affair, she "made it my business to go to my Brother's house and remonstrate" with Emiline about her conduct. Emiline, terrified and embarrassed, lashed out at Delia, who testified that the young woman "became very angry with me." After the rumors surfaced, neither Narcissa nor Delia wished to speak to Emiline, a noticeable occurrence because, prior to this, "scarcely three days elapsed without a visit" between them. But the rumors were vivid and verifiable enough that both of the Coleman sisters felt the need "to put a stop to all intimacy" with Emiline.

Emiline sensed the dangerous waters she had tread prior to her confrontation with Delia. The tryst with Henry Riley could destroy her life, and she responded to the possibility of discovery by attempting to break up with Henry through sad poetry:

Henry I love you
As in that joyous time
Henry, I ne'er will forget
Though memory now be crime
Henry, when fades the Light
Upon the Earth and Sea
I dream of you by night
You must not dream of me

She wrote several poems to Henry, often expressing an intense depression and a wish to die. Prior to her solitary attempt to end their affair, she penned a forlorn verse:

I am like the evening sun
That treats o'er the stormy sea
And o'ver billows curled,
That distant sounds decay,
I weep, and wish, from this rough world
Like them, to die away. Farewell.

On September 10, 1836, the day after Delia confronted Emiline, William W. Edwards worked at "a Stone Cutter's shop" that stood on a "vacant lott" owned by Judge Smith. The shop stood atop a hill on the other side of Randolph Street from John Coleman's house. From this elevated vantage point, the stonecutters watched what happened in his garden below. It was a Sunday, and around 3:00 p.m., "during the continuance of the afternoon service of the Methodist Church," William Edwards noticed people in the garden below.

He saw Emiline walk from Randolph Street into the back garden and continue onward to the "privy or necessary house." He made sure to take notice, because after watching "the maneuvers of Mrs Coleman and this man Riley" on several occasions, he was "almost certain that an improper intercourse was then existing" between them. His suspicions were confirmed. After she entered the privy, he saw Henry hop the fence separating the Colemans' house from the theater lot and join her inside.

John Coleman soon returned home. After tying his horse, Edwards witnessed him "take his seat near one of the windows with a Book" while Emiline and Riley continued their meeting in the outhouse. William Edwards was uncertain of how long they spent alone in their false seclusion, because he was ultimately a stonecutter and needed to return to cutting stone. He later came down from the shop and "met the said Riley in the street near Mr. Sydne's house." Edwards may have watched with humor

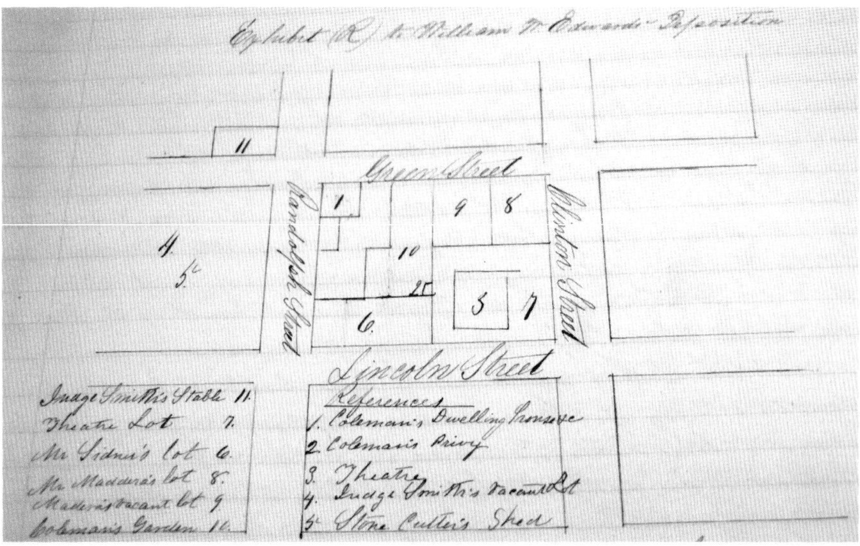

Street diagram. *Courtesy of the Madison County Probate Archives.*

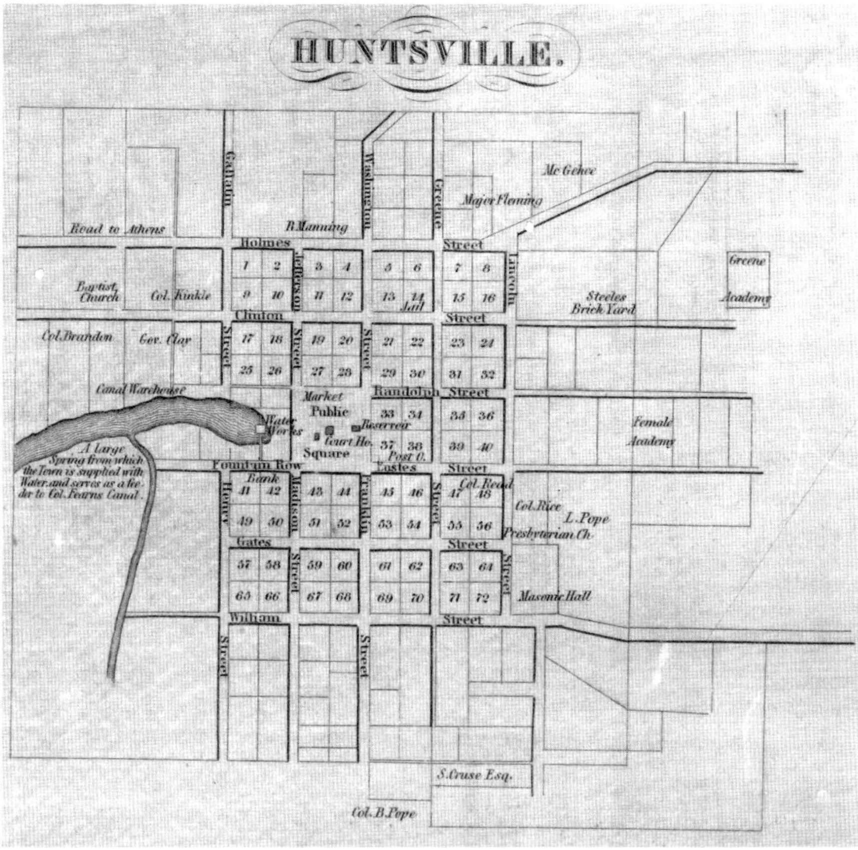

1840 map of Huntsville. *Courtesy of the Alabama Department of Archives and History.*

as Riley attempted to covertly exit the Colemans' lot and inconspicuously walk back to the theater.

Strangely enough, despite all their evidence, John's sisters never informed him of the rumors they'd gathered. It was Emiline's long absences in the garden that finally alerted him that something was amiss with his wife. After the incident with Delia, Emiline risked being caught with Henry Riley under the pretense of dawdling in the garden. While waiting for Riley to slink away, she spotted John and called out to him in an attempt to alert Riley of the imminent danger. On her return to the main dwelling house, John confronted her. John heard her speaking and said, "I must have known you," because "I stayed so very long." She denied everything. John pressed forward, asking her repeatedly who it was she spoke with in the garden. Emiline reported, "for the first time in his life he spoke unkind to me." He threatened to send her back to Greensboro, saying, "I might go my way and he would his." Finally, after several rounds of questioning, John saw that she would not speak and subsequently dropped the matter, but the later testimony of his friends shows that Emiline's increasingly erratic actions were enough to "rouse his suspicions."

Specifically, her loss of the picture. Years before, John Coleman had commissioned a small portrait of Emiline's likeness. In the midst of romantic passions, Emiline bequeathed it to Riley so that he might gaze on her visage while away. John later noticed the picture's absence and asked her where it went. Emiline scrambled for an explanation and settled on a strange one. She lied and "told him Miss Mary Crampton had it, and I hope God will forgive me for the lie." She went on to reveal to Riley that she felt hemmed in and "betrayed on every side" by her friends, family and the enslaved people in her household. All of the suspicion haunting her might dissipate—"if you will send the picture all will straight again."

Riley never returned the picture. In late September, she requested it again. He had left Huntsville, so he replied using a pseudonym in an effort to remain inconspicuous at the post office. Emiline would send an enslaved person to gather his letters, all addressed to an Edurina Johnson, and she would send letters to Mr. Cowell, an associate of Riley's in Huntsville who passed them along. This system worked so long as the courier remained uncompromised, but shortly after Riley's departure, one of the enslaved "carried [the letter] to Mr. C Sister." In it they discussed the picture, and either Narcissa or Delia informed John Coleman of his wife's loss of it. When confronted about it, Emiline lied. She must have proved convincing, because, once again, John Coleman withdrew his ire. Emiline ended this recounting to Riley with a simple warning: "never own that you had the picture."

In one of the letters she sent to Henry Riley pleading for the picture's return, she also mentioned sending money to Mary Crampton in the hopes that she would pass it all along to Riley. During their two-week affair, Emiline gave him cash, enclosed rings carved with her initials in the poetry she sent to him and risked her future and reputation—all for a little charm and understanding.

However, false charm cannot hold for long. On September 15, 1836, Riley planned to depart Huntsville. Based on addresses on the letters, it appears the company was returning to Tuscumbia or Muscle Shoals. Riley attempted to end the affair before he left.

Emiline did not take it well. When they met—for what Riley hoped was the last time—he said hateful things. He told her that he was "sorry I ever

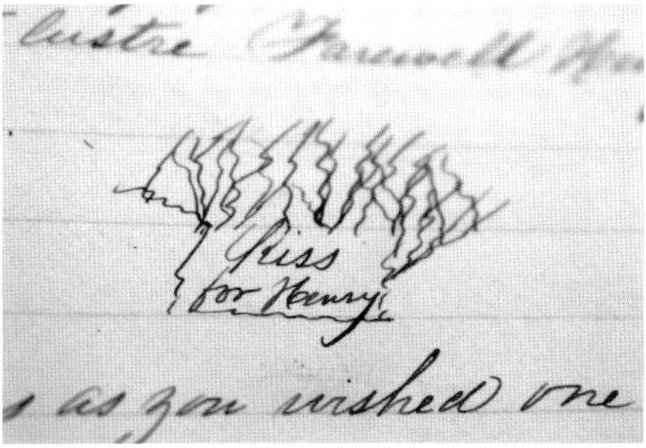

Kiss for Henry. *Courtesy of the Madison County Probate Archives.*

saw you" and wished she was dead. Emiline responded with a letter full of the morbid and tragic themes that purveyed her poetry. She warned him that "the time will come when I will be in the Tomb" and that, while the rest of the earth might remember her with peace and honor, "thou hast no tears to shed for me when I am at rest." Emiline continued in her despair: "You say that you wish I was dead," she wrote, "so you see I am willing." She dug in and informed the man who had taken her money, potentially ruined her reputation and told her he wished she was dead that "I wish I was only your wife."

Scorned by her lover and untrusted by her husband's family, Emiline withdrew to her family's home in Greene County to help care for her ailing mother. The experience was a hard one, and she coped by writing letters to Henry Riley in which she vividly described dreams she had. This was not the first time she described her dreams in letters to him. The day after he left Huntsville, she wrote at length about how angry John Coleman had become with her and how in a few years they might be "united with honor" upon his death. This letter noted a definite shift in her relationship with Riley. All previous letters had consisted of either brief instructions or poetry that balanced her fascination with death and her romanticizing of their future together. After Riley's departure, Emiline's letters became a rare window into the psyche of a young white woman in nineteenth-century Alabama.

In this first dream sequence, she described an encounter in a forest between herself and "the most beautiful child I thought that ever was." She described the boy as about four years old with glossy hair and "cheeks like roses." He led her to "his father's ship," and they set sail on a lake so smooth and calm that "like a mirror it was intirely unruffled." However, a storm cloud soon arose in the west. The lightning and thunder rocked the ship, and all seemed lost. The boy grasped her closely and begged Emiline to protect him. She asked him, before they were destined to die, who his father was. "Henry Riley is my father," the boy replied. Suddenly, Riley appeared onboard with them. In response to this good news, the storm abated and the ship righted itself. The experience was dramatic enough to wake Emiline, who remembered that she was alone in the house and "was mad it was a dream."

So, when she traveled to her family home in October 1836 to sit with her dying mother, it proved cathartic for her to pour out her emotions and dreams to an imagined version of Henry Riley who dwelt so far away. She described the setting in which she wrote: the whole house was asleep but "I alone am sitting watching oer my poor old mother." Emiline expressed her worry about the woman's fate and her failing health: "she is very ill indeed, it is past twelve o'clock the tears are streaming down my cheek now." Even in the midst of all this, she desired nothing more than to hear from Riley, who had not contacted her. She did not know "whether you are dead or alive."

With all this inner turmoil, she turned to describing her dreams again.

"If dreaming of you be crime my guilt is dark and deep," she began. In this rendition, she sat at home in her father's house adorned in "my bridal robes." She soon grew bored and left the home to venture down to the river with Ann. Emiline describes her excitement in leaving home and how she "tripped along with a fairy head" until they reached the river's edge. The sun hung low in the west, and the cliffs sparkled with "grandeur and sublimity." Emiline describes a beautiful scene, summarizing the imagined paradise of her dreams with a simple phrase: "Nature was now in its loveliest mood to me."

Across the riverbank she sighted an old man with a knapsack on his back and bearing his weight on a staff. The old man produced an instrument from the deep recesses of the knapsack and played "a wild and beautiful melody," which reminded her less of the music of man and more of the "far off voice of the roaring cataract." The old man, content with his music, then asked Emiline and Ann if they lived in the nearby mansion. They answered that they did. Next he said he was "lonely and weary" and wished to spend the night in a spare room. Emiline readily agreed. She leaned toward the old man to better hear him because "I loved to listen to the tones of the distressed."

It was then, while trying to hear the traveler, that she fell headlong into the river. The old man darted into the waves and pulled her back onto the riverbank. Confused about her rescuer, she turned to Ann and asked if this old man was secretly Henry Riley, but "she soon convinced me it was not you." The old man walked them back to the steps of her father's home so as to guard against further falls into raging waters. Emiline offered to take his things and keep them safe. She took his staff, his hat and his wallet. He turned to her and said, "here E take my wig." From under the gray locks of the wig appeared "the beautiful black hair" of Henry Riley. They embraced then, and her happiness was so powerful that she woke, only to find herself once again in a reality where she was sad and alone.

When Riley wrote to her next, it was not to profess his undying love but to ask for more favors. He told her of his many misfortunes in Tuscumbia and instructed her to write letters on his behalf to other men, namely ones he referred to as "T" and "F." She responded that she followed his instructions and that by the time he got this letter she would be back in Huntsville. She ended with a brief statement: "I was once a bright jewel but you have robbed me of its luster." Emiline still desperately wanted to believe in a better life for herself, especially one featuring Henry Riley, but his continuous inaction in coming to see her and constant requests for assistance had slowly turned her affections from giddy to gray.

December 17, 1836, was a Saturday, and at about 2:00 p.m., Preston Yeatman loaded salt onto a wagon. Yeatman was a prominent local merchant who served for a time on the Huntsville city council. He rented part of Judge Smith's brick stables on the corner of Randolph and Green Streets as a salthouse. The stables sat catercorner to the Coleman residence and provided an easy view of the goings-on of their household. John Lewis came and informed Yeatman that he had seen Henry Riley nearby. During Riley's previous stay in Huntsville, the men at the salthouse had heard the rumors about him and Emiline Coleman. So, they were intrigued by his "sudden and unlooked for reappearance…without any ostensible business" and began tracking his movements around the city. The two rushed to observe. They watched through the grates of the stable walls, a hiding spot that allowed them to view Riley walking down the street while they might "remain ourselves perfectly free from observation."

Riley passed by the Coleman residence. He stopped under a window and waited as "the window blinds of a window in the second story…cautiously opened and a small piece of paper" dropped down at his feet. Henry Riley then "cast around him a hasty glance" to see if anyone saw the exchange, picked up the paper so covertly dropped and "thrust it into the pocket of his pantaloons." Yeatman and Lewis watched him head toward the city center, where he might enjoy the relative safety and anonymity of the town square. The two men immediately rushed to find James McClung, a prosperous lawyer and well-known friend of John Coleman. They told him what they had seen.

Without hesitation, McClung crossed the street and roused John Coleman into action. He gathered their small posse—two lawyers, a merchant and

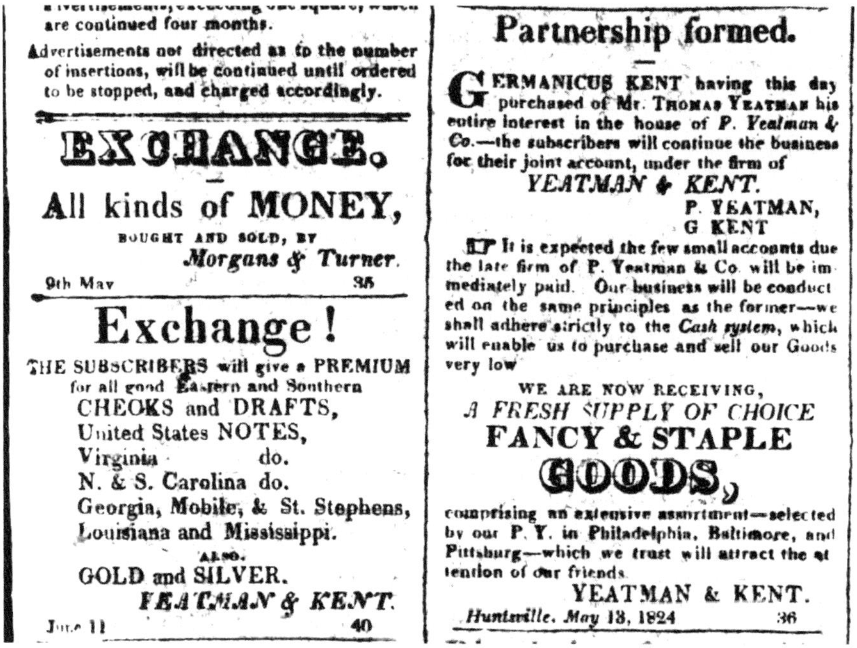

are continued four months.

Advertisements not directed as to the number of insertions, will be continued until ordered to be stopped, and charged accordingly.

EXCHANGE.

All kinds of MONEY,

BOUGHT AND SOLD, BY

Morgans & Turner.

9th May 35

Exchange!

THE SUBSCRIBERS will give a PREMIUM for all good Eastern and Southern

CHECKS and DRAFTS,
United States NOTES,
Virginia do.
N. & S. Carolina do.
Georgia, Mobile, & St. Stephens,
Louisiana and Mississippi.

ALSO.

GOLD and SILVER.

YEATMAN & KENT.

June 11 40

Partnership formed.

GERMANICUS KENT having this day purchased of Mr. THOMAS YEATMAN his entire interest in the house of *P. Yeatman & Co.*—the subscribers will continue the business for their joint account, under the firm of

YEATMAN & KENT.

P. YEATMAN,
G KENT

☞ It is expected the few small accounts due the late firm of P. Yeatman & Co. will be immediately paid. Our business will be conducted on the same principles as the former—we shall adhere strictly to the *Cash system*, which will enable us to purchase and sell our Goods very low

WE ARE NOW RECEIVING,

A FRESH SUPPLY OF CHOICE

FANCY & STAPLE

GOODS,

comprising an extensive assortment—selected by our P. Y. in Philadelphia, Baltimore, and Pittsburg—which we trust will attract the attention of our friends.

YEATMAN & KENT.

Huntsville, May 13, 1824 36

Preston Yeatman advert. *Courtesy of the Madison County Special Collections.*

the type of man with business in a salthouse—and informed them of his hasty plan. "I proposed to Mr. Coleman that we should seize Riley," James McClung admitted to the court, "and thus get possession of the paper." They set out to search for Riley in the "Public Square." They found him, and all four attempted to "seize" him, but the wily actor from Tuscumbia put up a fight. The men of Huntsville responded in kind. They recognized the four trying to search Riley, but they knew not the actor. So "with some assistance" from the general public, the four men "forcibly examined" him and found the latest note Emiline had penned in "his pantaloons pocket."

> *I am so much pleased to see you here once more but it is impossible for me to speak to you. I am still the same and ever shall be, return home Henry and forget me if you please, if it is ever in my power to become the Bride of H with honor I will, and as soon as I can you shall know it, keep my secret if you please, never betray me so long as you live, write a letter this evening and tonight after tea slip it through the window blinds of the porch. I will be there playing on the piano, Adieu Henry*
> *Yours—Yours*

Riley made a hasty exit from Huntsville after this, and Emiline Coleman was left to deal with the fallout alone. John Coleman did not immediately confront his wife; under Alabama divorce law, he could not even spend the night in the same house as her after learning of an affair. He found solace among friends at the local land office. Samuel Cruse listened to his tale of marital woe and, after "a long conversation," suggested they go to the Bell Tavern and search Riley's baggage.

Cruse and John Coleman found Mr. Caldwell, the owner of the Bell Tavern, and explained the situation. He allowed them into Riley's room, where they found his locked trunk. Caldwell objected to them "breaking said Trunk open," but they led the man out of the room and proceeded to forcibly search Riley's belongings. Inside the trunk they discovered one of his old playbills. It fell open to reveal a miniature portrait of Emiline Coleman and all the letters she ever wrote to Henry Riley.

Cruse paid for Emiline's passage back to Greensboro. She was chaperoned on the journey by Ann and a local judge named Reuben Nettles. From her perch, hundreds of miles away, she feebly contested the proceedings of the case against her. She claimed that Riley had stolen the portrait of her and that she wrote him a few letters demanding it back. All the love letters and poems were simply the work of "evil and designing persons" who wished to wreck her marriage and reputation because she refused to associate with them socially.[84]

All of her protests failed to counter the overwhelming evidence against her. On November 1, 1837, the court found Emiline guilty of adultery and granted John Coleman a full divorce against her.

CORNELIUS VERSUS CORNELIUS

On August 19, 1852, Emily Cornelius fled. She hid, not for the first time, among her neighbors and begged their protection from the man who beat her, William Cornelius, her husband.

Emily and William married on September 23, 1847, in Madison County. William was a rich man. He owned about 810 acres and counted among his property at least twenty slaves: Jim, Thirston, Chainey, Jules, Horace, Andy, Bake, Buck, Little, Jae, Bill, Dennis, Palena, Katy, Evilina, Solomon, Sarah, Jane, Charlotte, George, Larkin, Francis and an infant named Lena.

With his wealth and land—all derived from his surplus of slaves—William Cornelius achieved the status of planter, the rough-and-tumble elite of antebellum slave society. A planter, even a minor one like William Cornelius, wielded great and ugly power over his estate. Planters, free to terrorize and rape, rarely resembled the coiffed and dainty aristocrats of film and popular legend.

Due to this power and influence, and to their relative scarcity when weighed against the general population, we do not have many records of planter divorces in the antebellum South. Indeed, the normal circumstances for divorce rarely applied to them. Less wealthy white men who allowed a female slave to take their wife's place in bed might face a case, while planters' wives often lamented the existence of their husbands' sex slaves but usually ignored their presence. Planters had found fortune in their own counties and had no reason, like so many poor men, to shrug off the burdens of family and flee to Arkansas or the Republic of Texas. The few planter divorces on record are often the result of dramatic and brutal domestic violence.

For the first years of their marriage, William drank often. Emily described him as "addicted to the immoderate use of intoxicating drink," but all else was otherwise peaceful. Around 1850, his behavior changed. William Cornelius became "cruel, barbarous, & inhumane."

When he drank, he fell into the "frequent habit of heaping curses & imprecations of the most direful character" upon her. It quickly progressed from curses to shouted threats of violence and death. Then he started hitting her, delivering "violent blows with his fists & feet upon your oratrix." During the worst assaults, neighbors intervened to save her life.

Emily Cornelius began running from her husband. She counted at least four times prior to August 19, 1852. Each time she hid from him, William appeared later, sober and making "the most earnest asseverations…& uttering promises of the most solemn & sacred character" that he would quit drinking. Each time, she returned, convinced by his pleas, she might "hope for peace & happiness & safety in the discharge of her duties as a wife."

Each time, he lied. The tension built in their marriage, and he progressively used more extreme means of violence. In early June 1852, Emily Cornelius gave birth to a son, William Roland Cornelius—like his father. During her recovery period, when the infant was but three weeks old and she still feeble, William Cornelius attacked her. She cradled the infant in her arms while her husband "threatened to take the life of your oratrix if she opened her mouth." During the assault, William grabbed a chain and raised it to threaten her. He said he would kill her with it.

His mother, Ellen Cornelius, intervened. Ellen Cornelius moved between them and bodily shielded both Emily and the infant from her son's rage. For this, she "received a severe blow." Afterward, when William began to drink, they both hid.

On August 19, he confronted her in a drunken rage. This time, he brandished "an open Kine in his hand" and told her it was time for their "final separation." William told her to run and never come back, stating that if she returned, he would finally kill her. She fled. Emily took refuge with the neighbors and this time refused to return to her husband despite his pleadings.

In her suit, Emily Cornelius listed her total property as a slave named Harriet "about 14 years of age," who acted as a nurse for her infant son. She requested the court grant her a divorce, custody of William Roland Cornelius and a portion of her husband's ample estate as maintenance.

William Cornelius responded the same day. He affirmed that, yes, they had married in 1847, and he readily recognized that he was "addicted to the occasional immoderate use of intoxicating drinks" but protested at being called "an habitual drunkard." He said he wanted to quit drinking and wished longingly that "his morbid apetite for stimulants had permitted him to keep his oft renewed resolution of Amendment." He alleged that Emily knew about his problems with alcohol long before they got married and "they have become no worse since."

The response also implied that the marriage was a sham to get at William's money. He claimed that prior to the wedding he had been "in one of the worst paroxysms of intoxication of about a week's standing," and that during the actual ceremony he "was so much under the influence of liquor that he could scarcely stand."

William Cornelius framed the divorce proceedings as an elaborate ruse by Emily's father to get money to pay off his debts in Texas. His evidence for this was that her parents had been visiting during his most recent, and last, alleged assault and that she had spent much time with them. Despite all of these claimed machinations by herself and her family, William Cornelius contended that he held her in "tender regard" and simply wished for her to quit the divorce bill.

Abram Walker, the chancery court judge, saw all of this and issued his ruling on June 29, 1855. There would be no divorce, but William Cornelius would pay at least $1,000 in alimony and the infant should remain in Emily Cornelius's care. Although it did not grant her absolute autonomy, one can imagine Emily Cornelius finding temporary relief in this outcome.

It would be far too temporary. William appealed to the Alabama Supreme Court. In 1858, six years after Emily petitioned for divorce, strangers in Montgomery made a final declaration.[85]

George Washington Stone. *Courtesy of the Alabama Department of Archives and History.*

The remarks of Alabama Supreme Court justice George Stone summed up the difficulties the wives of planters faced when seeking equality before the law. Although Justice Stone readily admitted that when William Cornelius drank he became "a boisterous madman; [and] that these fits last for days," and that his violence required the intervention of neighbors to protect his wife and mother, the justice still thought that William was capable of reform. Poorer men who drank too much and assaulted their wives often had their marriages dissolved, but due to his wealth and stature, William retained future rights to his son when the boy no longer required "those tender offices that only a mother can bestow."

Although everyone knew of William Cornelius's temper and fondness for liquor and witnesses readily told of his cruelty toward Emily, he managed to parlay his wealth and power into good lawyers and supreme court appeals. Emily Cornelius appealed to the better nature of antebellum slave society and found none.

NOTES

Introduction

1. Anderson, "Models of Paleoindian and Early Archaic Settlement"; Futato, "A Synopsis of Paleoindian and Early Archaic Research in Alabama."
2. Walthall, *Prehistoric Indians of the Southeast Archaeology*, 116–31; Beck, "Regional Cults and Ethnic Boundaries in 'Southern Hopewell,'" 172.
3. Hoksbergen, "Phase II Archaeological Investigation of Site 1Ma1180"; Alexander, Kroulek, Trudeau and Lafferty III, "Phase III Data Recovery at Williams Springs Site (1MA1167)."
4. Smith, "Aboriginal Depopulation in the Postcontact Southeast"; Ramenofsky and Galloway, "Disease and the Soto Entrada."
5. Smith, "Aboriginal Depopulation in the Postcontact Southeast," 257; Worth, "Late Spanish Military Expeditions in the Interior Southeast."
6. Bowne, "'Carryinge awaye their Corne and Children'"; Ethridge, "Creating the Shatter Zone"; Fox, "Events as Seen from the North"; Gallay, *Indian Slave Trade*, 40–69; Galloway, "Confederacy as a Solution to Chiefdom Dissolution"; Jenkins, "Tracing the Origins of the Early Creeks"; Knight, "Formation of the Creeks"; Martin, "Southeastern Indians and the English Trade in Skins and Slaves."
7. 1777 Constitution, Vermont State Archives and Records Administration, accessed August 12, 2019; Knepper, *Official Ohio Lands Book*, 23–26; *Journals of the Continental Congress, 1774–1789,* ed. Ford et al., 33: 466–77; Lamplugh, "Yazoo Land Fraud"; Dupre, *Transforming the Cotton Frontier*, 16, 23–25; Haynes, *Mississippi Territory and the Southwest Frontier*, 2, 57.
8. "Chickasaw Treaty—1805," accessed August 12, 2019.
9. Dupre, *Transforming the Cotton Frontier,* 16–19; Southerland and Brown, *Federal Road through Georgia, the Creek Nation, and Alabama*, 11, 30; Hudson, *Creek Paths and Federal Roads*, 19–26.

10. Governor Williams to Secretary Gallatin, August 23, 1808, Document 966b, Series 488: Administration Papers, Mississippi Department of Archives and History, http://www.mdah.ms.gov/arrec/digital_archives/series/s488/detail/8990.
11. Secretary Gallatin to Governor Williams, November 8, 1808, Document 966c, Series 488: Administration Papers, Mississippi Department of Archives and History, http://www.mdah.ms.gov/arrec/digital_archives/series/s488/detail/8991; Proclamation of Governor Williams Creating Madison County, December 13, 1808, Document 966d, Series 488: Administration Papers, Mississippi Department of Archives and History, http://www.mdah.ms.gov/arrec/digital_archives/series/s488/detail/8992.
12. Territory-Wide Manufacturing Establishments and Manufacturers (Abstract), 1809, Series 486: Censuses, Mississippi Department of Archives and History, http://www.mdah.ms.gov/arrec/digital_archives/series/486/detail/35163.; Abstract of the Census for the Mississippi Territory for 1810, 1810, Series 486: Censuses, Mississippi Department of Archives and History, http://www.mdah.ms.gov/arrec/digital_archives/series/486/detail/35109.
13. Dupre, *Transforming the Cotton Frontier*, 26–34.
14. Taylor, *History of Madison County and Incidentally of North Alabama*, 120; James Carnes vs. Nathaniel Austin, Madison County, Alabama County Court Record Book 1, 1 2 (1810).
15. Royall, *Letters from Alabama on Various Subjects*, 28–52; "The Greatest Curiosity Now Exhibited in America. A Living Elephant," *Alabama Republican* (Huntsville, AL), October 23, 1819.
16. Table No. 2, Population of the United States in 1860: Alabama (U.S. Census Bureau, 1860), 8.

Chapter 1

17. Madison County, taxable property, 1812, Series 510: Territorial Tax Rolls, Mississippi Department of Archives and History, 6, http://www.mdah.ms.gov/arrec/digital_archives/series/510/detail/102044.
18. The Territory vs. John B. Haynes, Minute Book of Madison County Mississippi Territory of the Superior Court in Law and Equity, 1811–1819 (hereafter Minute Book), 20/18 (1811).
19. Madison County, taxable property, 1811, Series 510, 15, http://www.mdah.ms.gov/arrec/digital_archives/series/510/detail/102746; Madison County, taxable property, 1812, Series 510, 17, http://www.mdah.ms.gov/arrec/digital_archives/series/510/detail/102055; Madison County, taxable property, 1813, Series 510, 20, http://www.mdah.ms.gov/arrec/digital_archives/series/510/detail/102097.
20. Calvin & Gideon Morgan assignee of John B. Haynes vs. John Williams, Madison County, Alabama County Court Record Book (hereafter Record Book), 164–65 (1813); Robert McClaurine vs. John B. Haynes, Record Book, 176 (1813); John B. Haynes vs. David Paxton, Record Book, 257–58 (1813); Charles Cabaniss vs.

John B. Haynes, Record Book, 254–55 (1813); John Sanders vs. John B. Haynes, Record Book, 292–93 (1813); Stephen Neal assignee of Whites & Gilbreath vs. John B. Haynes, Record Book, 313–14 (1813); John C. Hamilton vs. John B. Haynes, Record Book, 321–322 (1813); John B. Haynes vs. John Lowrey, Record Book, 331–32 (1813).

21. The Territory vs. John B. Haynes, Minute Book, 184/148–185/149 (1814).

22. The Territory vs. John B. Haynes, Minute Book, 26/24–26/25 (1811); The Territory vs. John J. Winston, Minute Book, 31/29–32/29 (1811); The Territory vs. Anthony Winston, Minute Book, 42/35 (1812); The Territory vs. John J. Winston, Minute Book, 45/38 (1812).

23. John Winston assignee of John B. Haynes vs. John Eckford, Record Book, 220–21 (1813).

24. The Territory vs. Luther Morgan, Minute Book, 32/30 (1812).

25. Maxwell vs. Gilbreath, Record Book, 64–66 (1812).

26. Cullen Earp vs. William Badger, Record Book, 278–79 (1813).

27. William Wyatt vs. William Badger, Record Book, 104 (1813); Calvin & Giden Morgan assignee of John B. Haynes vs. Joseph Wofford, Record Book, 104–105 (1813).

28. Madison County, taxable property, 1812, Series 510, 25, http://www.mdah.ms.gov/arrec/digital_archives/series/510/detail/102063; Madison County, taxable property, 1813, Series 510, 35, http://www.mdah.ms.gov/arrec/digital_archives/series/510/detail/102112.

29. The Territory vs. William Gibson, Minute Book, 189/153–191/154 (1816); The Territory vs. Philip Fields, Minute Book, 192/155–193/156 (1816).

30. The Territory vs. John McMahan, Minute Book, 195/158–197/159 (1816); The Territory vs. Barnet Hicklin, Minute Book, 198/160–198/161 (1816); The Territory vs. William McMahan, Martin McMahan & Henry Seeman, Minute Book, 200/162 (1816).

31. The Territory vs. Byrd Ashburne, Minute Book, 201/163–204/166 (1816); The Territory vs. John Pate, Minute Book, 204/166–209/169 (1816).

32. The Territory vs. Clayton Talbot, Minute Book, 232/187–234/188 (1816); The Territory vs. John Milligan, Minute Book, 235/189–236–190 (1816); The Territory vs. Wm. W. Johnson, Minute Book, 237/191–238/192 (1816); The Territory vs. James Gordon, Minute Book, 238/192–240/193; "Ten Dollars Reward," *Madison Gazette* (Huntsville, AL), October 18, 1813.

33. The Territory vs. Thomas Evan, Minute Book, 282/232 (1818); The Territory vs. Thomas Evan, Minute Book, 284/233–285/234, (1818); The State vs. John C. McGehee, Madison County, Alabama, Superior & Circuit Court Record Book, 1819–1823, 11–12, (1818); The State vs. Livingston McGehee, Record Book, 1819–1823, 12 (1818).

34. The Territory vs. Richard Pryor, Record Book, 1819–1823, 16 (1817).

35. The State vs. Richard Prior, Record Book, 1819–1823, 82–83 (1820).

36. The State vs. Richard Pryor, Record Book, 1819–1823, 93 (1820); The State vs. Richard Prior, Record Book, 1819–1823, 179–80 (1822).

37. The State vs. Richard Prior, Record Book, 1819–1823, 189–90 (1820).

38. "Huntsville City Aldermen Minutes, February 1828–April 1832," Huntsville–Madison County Public Library, 37–38, 41, 57, 61, 87, 90, 155–57.
39. Rogers, *Apostles of Equality*, 57–58.
40. The State vs. Thomas Garner & Thomas Watson, Record Book, 1819–1823, 176–178 (1821); The State vs. Thomas McGehee, John Cottrell, & John Richardson, Record Book, 1819–1823, 77 (1821); The State vs. Anthony Metcalfe, Edward Morgan, Francis Morgan, Robert Jones & John McGaha, Record Book, 1819–1823, 79–80 (1821); The State vs. John Morgan, John Ingram, & Robert Jones, Record Book, 1819–1823, 81 (1821); The State vs. Thomas McGehee, Arthur Jones, & John Cottrell, Record Book, 1819–1823, 81–82 (1821); The State vs. John A. Cottrell, Record Book, 1819–1823, 94–95 (1822).
41. The State vs. Benjamin T. Saxon, John Stofford, & Robert Chapman, Record Book, 1819–1823, 125–126 (1822); The State vs. Benjamin Saxon, John Stofford, & Robert Chapman, Record Book, 1819–1823, 130–32 (1822); The State vs. Saxon et al, Record Book, 1819–1823, 178–79 (1822); The State vs. Benjamin T. Saxon, Record Book, 1819–1823, 215–16 (1822).

Chapter 2

42. The Territory vs. Eli Newman, Minute Book, 53/46–58/49 (1812).
43. The Territory vs. Samuel Steel, Record Book, 1811–1819, 90/75 (1812); "Chickasaw Agency 6th May 1817," *Alabama Republican*, August 5, 1817.
44. Dupre, *Transforming the Cotton Frontier*, 181–87.
45. "Election," *Alabama Republican*, October 29, 1824; The State vs. Edmond Lester, Andrew Lester, & Winbush Lester, Record Book, 1819–1823, 218–19 (1823); The State vs. Andrew Lester, Record Book, 1819–1823, 244–45 (1823); The State vs. Winbush Lester, Record Book, 1819–1823, 246–47 (1823).
46. The State vs. Burket Green, Record Book, 1819–1823, 170–73 (1821); The State vs. Daniel Rather, Record Book, 1819–1823, 150–51 (1823); The State vs. Burket Green, Record Book, 1819–1823, 127 (1823); Joseph Eastland to Governor Israel Pickens, July 3, 1823, ADAH.
47. The State vs. Philip Pritchett, Madison County, Alabama State Cases Record Book, 1852–1854, 1–11 (1852).

Chapter 3

48. *The Statutes of the Mississippi Territory, Revised and Digested by the Authority of the General Assembly*, ed. Harry Toulmin (Natchez, MS: Samuel Terrell, Printer to the Mississippi Territory, 1807), 385; "The Mississippi Constitution of 1817," Mississippi History Now, accessed September 14, 2019, http://www.mshistorynow.mdah.ms.gov/articles/98/index.php?s=extra&id=267; Alabama Constitution of 1819, accessed September 14, 2019, http://digital.archives.alabama.gov/cdm/ref/collection/legislature/id/213567.

49. The Territory vs. John Bell, Minute Book, 21/19–22/19 (1811).
50. Madison County, taxable property, 1812, Series 510, 23, http://www.mdah.ms.gov/arrec/digital_archives/series/510/detail/102061; Madison County, taxable property, 1813, Series 510, 27, http://www.mdah.ms.gov/arrec/digital_archives/series/510/detail/102104.
51. Madison County, taxable property, 1812, Series 510, 31, http://www.mdah.ms.gov/arrec/digital_archives/series/510/detail/102069.
52. The Territory vs. Randolph Rogers, Minute Book, 71/60–74/61 (1813).
53. The State vs. James E. Smith, Record Book, 1819–1823, 103–04 (1821).
54. The State vs. Andrew Wesson & Littleberry Wade & c, Record Book, 1819–1823, 200–02 (1823); The State vs. Williamson Land, Record Book, 1819–1823, 234–35 (1823); The State vs. Williamson Land, Record Book, 1819–1823, 235 (1823).

Chapter 4

55. "Arrival of the President," *Alabama Republican*, June 5, 1819.
56. "Convention," *Alabama Republican*, June 12, 1819; "The Republican," *Alabama Republican*, July 3, 1819.
57. "Celebration," *Alabama Republican*, July 8, 1819.
58. The State vs. Woody Martin, Record Book, 1819–1823, 2 (1819); The State vs. Daniel Murphy, Record Book, 1819–1823, 2–3 (1819); The State vs. James Badlem and William Badlem, Record Book, 1819–1823, 4 (1819).
59. The State vs. Giles G. Boggs, Record Book, 1819–1823, 69–70 (1821).
60. The State vs. Woody Martin, Record Book, 1819–1823, 128–129 (1823); The State vs. Woody Martin, Record Book, 1819–1823, 215 (1823).
61. The State vs. Philip Hoffman, Record Book, 1819–1823, 232–33 (1823); The State vs. Philip Hoffman, Record Book, 1819–1823, 233 (1823); The State vs. Philip Hoffman, Record Book, 1819–1823, 233–34 (1823).
62. The State vs. Stephen Neal, Record Book, 1819–1823, 95–96 (1822).
63. "An act to incorporate the City of Mobile," in *Acts of the General Assembly of the State of Alabama, Passed at Its First Session* (Huntsville, AL: John Boardman, 1820), 129; "An Act Amendatory to an act concerning Divorce," in *Acts Passed at the Sixth Annual Session of the General Assembly of the State of Alabama* (Cahawba, AL: William B. Allen, Printer to the State, 1825), 61.
64. "An Act Regulating Punishments Under the Penitentiary System," in *Acts Passed at the Annual Session of the General Assembly of the State of Alabama* (Tuscaloosa, AL: Hale & Phelan, 1840), 124.
65. The State vs. Rodah Barnett, Mary King, Mary Baker, Barbary Wilson, Ann Martin, Elizabeth Burton & Lucinda Wilson, Record Book, 1819–1823, 34–35 (1820).
66. The State vs. David Davis, Record Book, 1819–1823, 86–87 (1821).
67. The State vs. Mary Baker, Mary King, & Ann Martin, Record Book, 1819–1823, 49–50 (1820).
68. The State vs. Rodah Barnett, Record Book, 1819–1823, 93–94 (1821).
69. The State vs. Elizabeth King, Record Book, 1819–1823, 100–02 (1821).

70. The State vs. Jenning Seay, Record Book, 1819–1823, 50 (1820); The State vs. Jeremiah Murphy & Lawrence Pendergrass, Record Book, 1819–1823, 149–50 (1823).
71. The State vs. Robert Smith, Mary Pratt, Francis Pratt, & Henry Ray, Record Book, 1819–1823, 42–43 (1821); The State vs. John Smith & Sarah Walker, Record Book, 1819–1823, 43 (1821); The State vs. Fanny Cark & Robert Smith, Record Book, 1819–1823, 90–91 (1822); The State vs. Robert Smith & others, Record Book, 1819–1823, 104 (1821).
72. John Thanor vs. Angelina Thanor, Madison County, Alabama Chancery Court Record Book K, 449–54 (1840); Sally Rountree vs. William Rountree, Chancery Court Record Book A, 359–61 (1823).
73. The State vs. Charles T. Collins, Record Book, 1819–1823, 24–25 (1820); The State vs. Charles T. Collins, Record Book, 1819–1823, 25–26 (1820); The State vs. Charles T. Collins, Record Book, 1819–1823, 26 (1820); The Territory vs. Thomas K. Roberts and Nicholas Sheffield, Minute Book, 254/207–255/208 (1817).
74. James Blair vs. William Wilborn, Madison County, Alabama, County Court Record Book, 1811–1813, 48–49 (1811); James Burlison vs. William Wilborn, Record Book, 1811–1813, 51–52 (1810); William Wilborn vs. James Burlison, Record Book, 1811–1813, 53–54 (1812).
75. Claiborne Griffin vs. Jesse Daniel, Record Book, 1811–1813, 72–73 (1812); Jesse Daniel vs. Claiborne Griffin, Record Book, 1811–1813, 73 (1812).
76. The Territory vs. William Blevins, Record Book, 1811–1819, 50/44 (1812); The Territory vs. Isaac Parrot, Record Book, 1811–1819, 219/177–220/178 (1816).

Chapter 5

77. Schweninger, *Families in Crisis in the Old South*, ix–xv, 1–16; Riley, *Divorce*, 3–17, 25–44.
78. Madison County, taxable property, 1811, Series 510, 24, http://www.mdah.ms.gov/arrec/digital_archives/series/510/detail/102755; Madison County, taxable property, 1813, 40, http://www.mdah.ms.gov/arrec/digital_archives/series/510/detail/102117.
79. Jones-Rogers, *They Were Her Property*, ix–5.
80. Wm. Rountree vs. Sally Rountree, Chancery Court Record Book A, 212–14 (1822); Sally Rountree vs. William Rountree, Chancery Court Record Book A, 359–61 (1823).
81. Mary Hall vs. Nathaniel Hall, Chancery Court Record Book K, 211–48 (1838); Nathaniel Hall vs. Polly Hall, Chancery Court Record Book L, 171–72 (1842).
82. Buchan, *Domestic Medicine*, 187, 365, 417.
83. John Layman vs. Rebecca Layman, Chancery Court Record Book D, 252–54 (1827).
84. John J. Coleman vs. Emiline R. Coleman, Chancery Court Record Book J, 91–114 (1837).
85. Censer, "'Smiling Through Her Tears,'" 44; Emily Cornelius by her next friend Robert True vs. William Cornelius, Chancery Court Record Book V, 605–18 (1852).

BIBLIOGRAPHY

Archives, Manuscripts and Other Primary Sources

Acts of the General Assembly of the State of Alabama, Passed at Its First Session. Huntsville, AL: John Boardman, 1820.

Acts Passed at the Annual Session of the General Assembly of the State of Alabama. Tuscaloosa, AL: Hale and Phelan, 1840.

Acts Passed at the Sixth Annual Session of the General Assembly of the State of Alabama. Cahawba, AL: William B. Allen, 1825.

Alabama. 1860 U.S. Census. Population Schedule.

Alabama Constitution of 1819. Alabama Department of Archives and History. http://digital.archives.alabama.gov.

Alabama Department of Archives and History.

Buchan, William. *Domestic Medicine: Or a Treatise on the Prevention and Cure of Diseases by Regimen and Simple Medicines*. London: A. Strahan, 1784.

"Chickasaw Treaty—1805." The Avalon Project, Lillian Goldman Law Library. Accessed August 12, 2019. https://avalon.law.yale.edu.

Huntsville–Madison County Public Library Special Collections and Probate Archive. Huntsville City Aldermen Minutes, February 1828–April 1832.

———. Madison County, Alabama Chancery Court Record Book A.

———. Madison County, Alabama Chancery Court Record Book D.

———. Madison County, Alabama Chancery Court Record Book J.

———. Madison County, Alabama Chancery Court Record Book K.

———. Madison County, Alabama Chancery Court Record Book L.

———. Madison County, Alabama Chancery Court Record Book V.

———. Madison County, Alabama County Court Record Book, 1811–1813.

———. Madison County, Alabama State Cases Record Book, 1852–1854.

———. Minute Book of Madison County, Mississippi Territory of the Superior Court in Law and Equity, 1811–1819.

Journals of the Continental Congress, 1774–1789. Edited by Worthington C. Ford, et al. Washington, D.C., 1904–1937.

"The Mississippi Constitution of 1817." *Mississippi History Now*. Accessed September 14, 2019. http://www.mshistorynow.mdah.ms.gov.

Mississippi Department of Archives and History. Administration Papers, 1769, 1788–1817. http://www.mdah.ms.gov.

———. Censuses, 1801–1816. http://www.mdah.ms.gov.

———. Territorial Tax Rolls, 1802–1817. http://www.mdah.ms.gov.

Royall, Ann Newport. *Letters from Alabama on Various Subjects.* Washington, D.C., 1830.

Toulmin, Harry *The Statutes of the Mississippi Territory.* Natchez, MS: Samuel Terrell, 1807.

Vermont State Archives and Records Administration. 1777 Constitution. https://www.sec.state.vt.us.

Newspapers

Alabama Republican (Huntsville, Alabama)

Madison Gazette (Huntsville, Mississippi Territory)

Southern Advocate (Huntsville, Alabama)

Secondary

Alexander, Lawrence S., Orion S. Kroulek, Mary F. Trudeau and Robert H. Lafferty III. "Phase III Data Recovery at Williams Springs Site (1MA1167), a Late Middle Woodland Village on Redstone Arsenal, Madison County, Alabama." ResearchGate. Environmental Management Support, 2017. https://www.researchgate.net.

Anderson, David G. "Models of Paleoindian and Early Archaic Settlement in the Lower Southeast." In *The Paleoindian and Early Archaic Southeast*, edited by David G. Anderson and Kenneth E. Sassaman, 29–58. Tuscaloosa: University of Alabama Press, 1996.

Beck, Lane Anderson. "Regional Cults and Ethnic Boundaries in 'Southern Hopewell.'" In *Regional Approaches to Mortuary Analysis*, edited by Lane Anderson Beck, 167–84. New York: Plenum Press, 1995.

Bowne, Eric E. ""Carryinge awaye their Corne and Children": The Effects of Westo Slave Raids on the Indians of the Lower South." In *Mapping the Mississippian Shatter Zone: The Colonial Indian Slave Trade and Regional Instability in the American South*, edited by Robbie Ethridge and Sheri M. Shuck-Hall, 104–14. Lincoln: University of Nebraska Press, 2009.

Censer, Jane Turner. "'Smiling Through Her Tears': Antebellum Southern Women and Divorce." *American Journal of Legal History* 25, no. 1 (1981): 24–47.

Dupre, Daniel S. *Transforming the Cotton Frontier: Madison County, Alabama, 1800–1840.* Baton Rouge: Louisiana State University Press, 1997.

Ethridge, Robbie. "Creating the Shatter Zone: Indian Slave Traders and the Collapse of the Southeastern Chiefdoms." In *Light on the Path: The Anthropology and History of the Southeastern Indians*, edited by Thomas J. Pluckhahn and Robbie Ethridge, 207–17. Tuscaloosa: University of Alabama Press, 2006.

Fox, William A. "Events as Seen from the North: The Iroquois and Colonial Slavery." In *Mapping the Mississippian Shatter Zone: The Colonial Indian Slave Trade and Regional Instability in the American South*, edited by Robbie Ethridge and Sheri M. Shuck-Hall, 63–80. Lincoln: University of Nebraska Press, 2009.

Futato, Eugene M. "A Synopsis of Paleoindian and Early Archaic Research in Alabama." In *The Paleoindian and Early Archaic Southeast*, edited by David G. Anderson and Kenneth E. Sassaman, 298–315. Tuscaloosa: University of Alabama Press, 1996.

Gallay, Alan. *The Indian Slave Trade: The Rise of the English Empire in the American South, 1670–1717.* New Haven, CT: Yale University Press, 2002.

Galloway, Patricia. "Confederacy as a Solution to Chiefdom Dissolution: Historical Evidence in the Choctaw Case." In *The Forgotten Centuries: Indians and Europeans in the American South, 1521–1704*, edited by Charles Hudson and Carmen Chaves Tesser, 393–420. Athens: University of Georgia Press, 1994.

Haynes, Robert V. *The Mississippi Territory and the Southwest Frontier, 1795–1817.* Lexington: University Press of Kentucky, 2010.

Hoksbergen, Ben. "Phase II Archaeological Investigation of Site 1Ma1180, a Wetland Margin Late Woodland Flint River Component on Redstone Arsenal, Madison County, Alabama." ResearchGate. Environmental Management Division, Garrison-Redstone Arsenal. 2011. https://www.researchgate.net.

Hudson, Angela Pulley. *Creek Paths and Federal Roads: Indians, Settlers, and Slaves in the Making of the American South.* Tuscaloosa: University of Alabama Press, 2010.

Jenkins, Ned J. "Tracing the Origins of the Early Creeks, 1050–1700 CE." In *Mapping the Mississippian Shatter Zone: The Colonial Indian Slave Trade and Regional Instability in the American South*, 188–249. Lincoln: University of Nebraska Press, 2009.

Jones-Rogers, Stephanie E. *They Were Her Property: White Women as Slave Owners in the American South.* New Haven, CT: Yale University Press, 2019.

Knepper, George W. *The Official Ohio Lands Book.* Columbus: Auditor of the State of Ohio, 2002.

Knight, Vernon James. "The Formation of the Creeks." In *The Forgotten Centuries: Indians and Europeans in the American South, 1521–1704*, edited by Charles Hudson and Carmen Chaves Tesser, 373–92. Athens: University of Georgia Press, 1994.

Lamplugh, George R. "Yazoo Land Fraud." New Georgia Encyclopedia, revised June 8, 2017. Accessed August 12, 2019. https://www.georgiaencyclopedia.org.

Martin, Joel W. "Southeastern Indians and the English Trade in Skins and Slaves." In *The Forgotten Centuries: Indians and Europeans in the American South, 1521–1704*, edited by Charles Hudson and Carmen Chaves Tesser, 304–24. Athens: University of Georgia Press, 1994.

Ramenofsky, Ann F., and Patricia Galloway, "Disease and the Soto Entrada," in *The Hernando de Soto Expedition: History, Historiography, and "Discovery" in the Southeast*, edited by Patricia Galloway, 259–79. Lincoln: University of Nebraska Press, 2005.

Riley, Glenda. *Divorce: An American Tradition.* New York: Oxford University Press, 1991.

Rogers, D. Laurence. *Apostles of Equality: The Birneys, Republicans, and the Civil War.* East Lansing: Michigan State University Press, 2011.

Schweninger, Loren. *Families in Crisis in the Old South: Divorce, Slavery, and the Law.* Chapel Hill: University of North Carolina Press, 2012.

———. "'To the Honorable': Divorce, Alimony, Slavery, and the Law in Antebellum North Carolina." *North Carolina Historical Review* 84 (2009): 127–79.

Smith, Marvin T. "Aboriginal Depopulation in the Postcontact Southeast." In *The Forgotten Centuries: Indians and Europeans in the American South, 1521–1704*, edited by Charles Hudson and Carmen Chaves Tesser, 257–76. Athens: University of Georgia Press, 1994.

Southerland, Henry Jr., and Jerry Elijah Brown. *The Federal Road through Georgia, the Creek Nation, and Alabama, 1806–1836.* Tuscaloosa: University of Alabama Press, 1989.

Taylor, Thomas Jones. *A History of Madison County and Incidentally of North Alabama, 1732–1840.* Edited by W. Stanley Hoole and Addie S. Hoole. University, AL: Confederate Publishing Company, 1976.

Walthall, John A. *Prehistoric Indians of the Southeast Archaeology of Alabama and the Middle South.* Tuscaloosa: University of Alabama Press, 2010.

Watson, Donald F. *Printed Acts of Alabama, 1818–1864.* Montgomery: Alabama Department of Archives and History, 1971.

Worth, John E. "Late Spanish Military Expeditions in the Interior Southeast, 1597–1628." In *The Forgotten Centuries: Indians and Europeans in the American South, 1521–1704*, edited by Charles Hudson and Carmen Chaves Tesser, 104–22. Athens: University of Georgia Press, 1994.

ABOUT THE AUTHOR

John O'Brien is a hopeful writer currently living in North Alabama. Long fascinated by the long ago, he spends his free time looking at old records so he can more effectively gossip about dead people. John runs a blog about North Alabama history called Huntsvillain. You can find it on the internet and Facebook. When in public, he is instructed in normalcy by his long-suffering and much beloved wife, who often tells him that not everyone wishes to hear about the health of local swamps. This is his second rodeo.